MORE
MR. FRO⎯⎯⎯
BARKING

A SECOND SELECTION

TONY CLIFFORD & HERBERT HOPE LOCKWOOD

A personal history of Barking at
the beginning of the 20th Century

The London Borough of
Barking & Dagenham

2003

Cover picture: An oilette postcard of
the boating lake in Barking Park, circa 1900.

PREFACE

I am very pleased to introduce this second selection from the manuscript of William Holmes Frogley. The first selection of extracts related mainly to the old town centre of Barking and its principal industries at that time - fishing and the jute works. The second selection reminds us of the agricultural basis of the local economy. Agriculture was predominant from the earliest times right through to the outward expansion of Barking and the building of the Becontree housing estate which swept away the gentry estates and the farming community. Here is an invaluable record of an organic community from a world we have lost.

Frogley lived at Windsor Cottage, 44 Longbridge Road. The house still exists - a photograph is included in this book. It overlooks a brand new arrival in Barking Town Centre - The Catch, a public artwork designed by the artist Loraine Leeson of cSPACE in collaboration with Anne Thorne Architects Partnership and built by Alloy Fabweld Ltd. The artwork reflects two key elements of Barking's heritage and history - the fishing industry and the area's Saxon heritage. It is interesting to imagine what Frogley would have thought of this monument to an industry that was very close to his heart and which was the occupation of his ancestors. We have not completely lost touch with our past.

I would like to end by taking the opportunity to thank Tony Clifford for his tireless work in bringing the acute and often astringent observations of William Holmes Frogley to life. Without his dedication this candid introduction to the history of Barking at the start of the twentieth century would remain hidden in an inaccessible manuscript. The Frogley manuscript is of such importance that at least one more book will be produced. There is much to look forward to - and much more work for Tony to do. I am sure he will enjoy doing it and we will benefit greatly from his efforts.

Roger Luxton

Director of Education, Arts & Libraries,
London Borough of Barking & Dagenham

INTRODUCTION

Welcome to "Frogley 2", the second selection from the manuscript history of Barking written by William Holmes Frogley (1855-1924) between the mid 1890s to just before the First World War. The first selection concentrated on the town centre and the fishing industry. The extracts transcribed and reproduced here mainly cover Barking's agricultural past, an inventory of memorials in the churchyard, and the development of non-conformist religious bodies, which were so prominent and influential in the town. The development of estates such as Westbury and Bifrons are described, the contemporary perspective being enhanced by historical detail gathered from a variety of sources.

Why have we provided so many footnotes? These are necessary to corroborate or correct Frogley's contemporary account, using commercial directories and other sources. They give extra information about the topic, place or individual under discussion whenever we can provide this. They also give us the opportunity to correct mistakes made by Frogley or his collaborator(s), for example in the section dealing with the memorials in Barking churchyard[1]. There is some evidence to suggest that Frogley was not alone in compiling this account of his home town, and that he also checked his associates' information.

An ongoing source of enquiry is to find out where Frogley managed to find copies of the books to which he refers[2]. A public lending library opened in Barking in 1889, the first in Essex, with a stock of 700 books and a small reference section[3]. This cannot have been where Frogley consulted his sources. However, George Jackson, the first librarian, is described as a friend; perhaps this was his route to the information he quotes. Our footnotes give details of some of Frogley's sources. They could only have been available to him in established collections such as the Guildhall Library, or perhaps in the private collections of local historians such as William Wallis Glenny.

In the introduction to our first selection, Bert Lockwood gives a lot of information regarding William Holmes Frogley, his family and ancestors.

---

1 Bert Lockwood has compared Frogley's listing with the 1930 survey of memorials in St Margaret's churchyard and the burial registers, with often surprising inconsistencies.

2 See *Mr Frogley's Barking: a first selection.* 2002. p.10-11.

3 Alan Hill: *One hundred years of libraries in Barking: a centenary report.* 1989.

MORE OF MR FROGLEY'S BARKING: A SECOND SELECTION

The five generations of Barking Frogleys traced by Bert and other researchers take us back to Joseph (b.1740) who married Jane Wells (b.1739) in 1764. Nothing new has come to light as a result of "Frogley 1", despite posting messages on web sites world-wide such as the Frogley Family Genealogy Forum[4]. Frogley is not a common name and they appear rarely in documents. For example, Arthur Frogley, probably a Cambridgeshire man[5], made a survey of a farm in Hatfield Broad Oak in July 1714[6]. In the same month and year he was a witness to an incursion into the highway at Plaistow[7]. He was also responsible for an undated, roughly executed map of part of the parish of Ramsey belonging to a local freeholder[8]. We do not yet know if Arthur was related to our William Holmes Frogley.

In this second selection we have repeated for the benefit of the reader the notes on transcription from "Frogley 1". We have to report that there has been no corroboration of the handwriting, although there is no reason to dispute that the manuscript acquired by Fred Brand is not the author's neat copy made from notes gathered from a wide variety of sources. The index referred to on page 11 of "Frogley 1" is due to be published on CD-ROM by the East of London Family History Society, in early 2003, along with a facsimile of the original. This will be a very welcome accompaniment to these transcriptions. The plan for "Frogley 3" is to transcribe more of the manuscript, but to include also an index to all the text transcribed to date. It is unlikely that the chunks of text copied from standard histories available to Frogley – for example, the section relating to Barking abbey – will be included in this series.

---

4 http://genforum.genealogy.com/frogley
5 See A. Stuart Mason: *Essex on the map: the 18th century land surveyors of Essex.* 1990. p.39.
6 Essex Record Office D/DXa 22 (the marshes) and D/DGe P8 (Tillingham Hall).
7 Essex Record Office D/DEt/P6.
8 Essex Record Office D/P 339/3/5.

Notes on transcription.

The family of the author of this manuscript lived in Barking for at least five generations and were related to many local tradesmen. William Holmes Frogley (1855-1924) - we are now certain of the author's identity - was clearly educated to a reasonable standard. Although not written or illustrated with professional polish, this account of Barking from the mid 1890s to just before the First World War accurately records its subject matter. This is confirmed in the footnotes, which are intended to match up the author's descriptions with other contemporary records, such as commercial directories of Essex (which at that time included Barking). The author takes us on a conducted tour of Barking, describing many buildings which have now disappeared. He shows us glimpses of the past and introduces us to the inhabitants of the town. It is a wonderful example of one man's obsession with recording the history of his native town.

The handwriting in the manuscript is generally neat and easy to read, although tiny on occasion. To put investigations on a more scientific basis, we need to find other material written by William Holmes Frogley to compare with this manuscript. We also need the opinion of a handwriting expert to confirm whether the manuscript is the work of a single person, or several.

Throughout this narrative I have tried to retain the author's original spelling and grammar, to preserve the historical context and the spirit of the narrative. Faced with the option of changing whatever was necessary to suit contemporary usage and vocabulary, I originally decided to apply a few simple insertions to make the text more approachable to the modern reader, whilst preserving the content of the author's manuscript. On later reflection, this made the text too complicated to read, and I soon abandoned this approach.

There are consistent mistakes in the use of grammar; for example, the use of "was" as a plural instead of "were", and virtually no use of apostrophes. Extremely long sentences and paragraphs are often stringed together by using "&"s, hyphens and other punctuation, which causes havoc with modern electronic grammar checkers, the use of which I more or less gave up on.

Square brackets – [ ] – have been used whenever any query or alteration of the original text has been required. For example, there are sometimes gaps in the text where a word or date has been omitted, for whatever reason, and I have indicated this with "[ ]". I have used round brackets – ( ) – whenever the author has used them in the text; they also indicate the insertion of a relevant footnote from the original manuscript into the appropriate point in the text. Very rarely, I have missed out text because of repetition, duplication, irrelevancy, or because it will be included in a future booklet in this series; this is indicated by [...].

Interjections and asides are frequent in the manuscript, and the concluding comma or hyphen of the inserted text is often omitted by the author. I have inserted the missing punctuation for ease of reading. There is frequent use of "&c" in lists, the equivalent of the modern "etc". This sometimes develops into "&c &c" or even "&c &c &c".

Frogley makes frequent use of capital letters in nouns. Perhaps some extra emphasis or importance is intended with regard to certain trades, professions and activities by giving them a leading capital letter. "Auction" is a typical example, and perhaps gives a clue as to how he may have obtained some of the information in the book. In particular, any trade connected with the fishing industry usually has a capital letter, and he clearly has a great affection for this part of Barking's history, in which his family was involved for many generations. He was clearly not in favour of any of the "improvements" inflicted on the town by the railway, and usually prefixes any account of them with "so-called".

I have drawn heavily from this manuscript in my own books and articles, and it has been a real pleasure carrying out the transcription and research for this book. I am delighted that the contents will now be available to a wider audience.

Tony Clifford

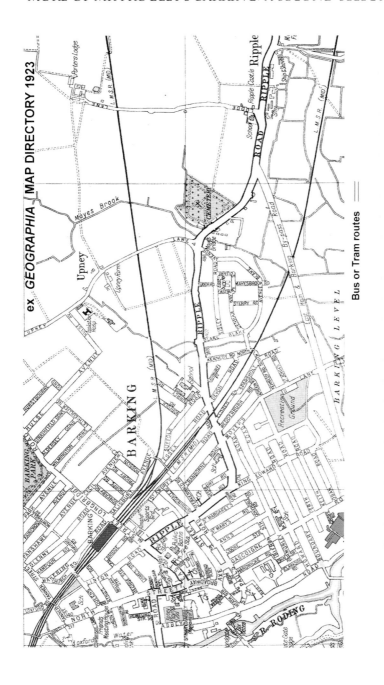

Longbridge-Road [Pages 456-464]

This road until recent years was really a lane and a favorite walk for young couples. It is a continuation of East Street leading to the Green Lanes, Ilford & thence to Romford. Previous to 1880 I beleive that there was no more – if so many – as 12 houses from one end to the other, but since that date it has undergone a great change as will be seen. Starting from the Station -–on the right hand side was open fields to Faircross Farm. Almost adjoining the railway was a peice of land purchased by the "Methodists" for a new Chapel but they sold it & a few houses was built on it. These were demolished for Railway extension.

Stoney-Road (now   ) was a pathway leading from Longbridge Road to the Ripple Road, accross the Farm occupied by Mr W. W. Glenny[1].

1   William Wallis Glenny (1839-1923), according to one obituary, "worked quietly and unostentatiously in the discharge of his many activities, and no one could have been more esteemed alike by his colleagues, the officials, and indeed, all who have been brought into contact with him, to whom he ever displayed the greatest courtesy and kindliness". His first office was taken up in 1864, when he became a member of the Romford Board of Guardians, a capacity in which he served for 30 years. From 1872 to 1893 he was Chairman of the Board and of the Assessment Committee, which made a great demand on his time. In 1880 he became a Justice of the Peace and regularly attended at the courts. In 1889, he was elected without opposition as Barking's representative on Essex County Council. In local affairs he was particularly interested in educational matters, and was chosen as the first Chairman of Barking School Board; he presided over the Education Committee until 1918. For a considerable period he was master and manager of the Barking Savings Bank, and was also one of the Barking Charity Trustees and an active member of the Commissions of Sewers.

Farmers Weekly, August 24, 1973 contained an article "Winning ways in Victorian days", which describes W. W. Glenny's farming methods: "The Royal Agricultural Society of England in 1879 organised a competition to encourage farmers in the London area to grow more vegetables. The idea was to bring a better supply of these almost essential elements of food within the reach not only of the artisans, mechanics and workers of all kinds who rarely can get them, but also of the very many members of what are styled the lower middle classes dwelling in London and other cities and towns, in whose households fresh vegetables are almost equally scarce commodities. It aimed to show farmers that they might profitably add the culture of at least the most hardy and most easily grown vegetables to their usual routine of farm production. Winner of the section for the "best market farm above 100 acres and within 50 miles of the Mansion House" was South Hall Market Garden Farm at Rainham, Essex. Second prize for a garden farm went to William Wallis Glenny, who had 208 acres at Barking. The soil was clay or loamy clay of medium quality 3-4 ft deep and resting on a gravelly subsoil. Geographically the farm was in three divisions - one part near Mr. Glenny's house and homestead in Barking, another nearly a mile away to the north-east and the third half-a-mile from Barking. The homestead section was cropped mainly with corn alternated with

9

(The land formerly belonged to G. Glenny Esqr who died in 1839[2] & bequeathed it to his brother Alexander[3] & his sisters Elizbeth, Mary[4] & Sarah & at their death to his brother William[5]. But Mary outlived all four, dying in 18— unmarried. (William died 1850). Marys age at her death was 8.

vegetables, the one farthest away with wheat, oats, potatoes and mangels [kind of beet used as cattle food], and the area south of Barking given over to the more usual market garden crops.

At the time of the judges' inspection, Mr. Glenny was marketing high-quality East Ham cabbages and Lisbon onions. The onions were sent in bunches containing as much as a man could hold in both hands, spread out in a fan shape and packed in layers in baskets. Gross return was £60 to £70 an acre. Peas, carrots and broad beans followed the onions to market and after that early potatoes. Mr. Glenny, like most market gardeners of the period, sold the potatoes as soon as they were ready. After the potatoes came scarlet runner and French beans, marrows and cucumbers. Favourite potato varieties were Red Bog, Champion and Dalmahoy, most of the seed coming from Scotland. Immunity or near-immunity from potato blight was obtained by planting early potatoes, which were dug as soon as possible so that the blight did not get a chance to develop. Peas were mostly Fortyfold, Fill-basket, William the First and Dr. Maclean. There was also a fine show of Broad Windsor beans, for podding, which were set 18 in apart and earthed-up like potato plants to protect the stems and keep them standing erect. Mr. Glenny grew a large amount of scarlet runner beans but that year he was obliged to plough up several acres as the seed had rotted in the ground. The wet season had made carrot weeding difficult, for no sooner did the men hoe them over but it rained and weeds came again. Slugs ate so many parsnips in one patch that it had to be ploughed in. Normally the parsnips were not dug until wanted for the market, for it was held that staying in the ground sweetened them. Some years it was possible to keep the parsnips in the ground until Lent, when there was a good demand for them to go with the Lenten fish.

The buildings on Mr. Glenny's farm were marked by the judges as "good and in excellent repair." Nearly everything in the way of repairs was done on the farm, also the making of new implements. Fourteen horses occupied the roomy, well-ventilated stables and others were hired during the busy season. Steam ploughing and cultivating tackle was usually hired. Two or three cows were kept and several sows of the Large White breed, which had been crossed with a Berkshire boar. These more or less lived off vegetable waste".

2   George Glenny (1772-1839) was the 5th son of Alexander Glenny (d.1782) of Cobb Hall, founder of the Barking dynasty. He farmed with brother William and died unmarried. He is the only Glenny with a memorial in St Margaret's Church, Barking. He was Guardian, 1827-30 and Surveyor, 1808-11. *Barking vestry minutes*. 1955. p.42.

3   Alexander Glenny (1765-1843) was blinded as a child, but still managed to play the organ at St Margaret's and other churches. He married, but probably died childless.

4   Mary Glenny went to live with her elder brother, John, who farmed in Battersea. She died in 1856, and was buried at Barking. For further information about the Glenny family see: *Mr Frogley's Barking: a first selection*. 2002. p.132-136 and associated footnotes.

5   William Glenny (1766-1850) was the 3rd son of Alexander Glenny. He was Churchwarden, 1809-37; Overseer, 1804; and Surveyor, 1810. *Barking vestry minutes*. 1955. p.42.

The Land remained in the Glenny Family). The first portion of Land sold in this Road was the front portion, extending from Stoney Road to Faircross Farm or beyond. The length of it was 1262 feet and a depth from the Longbridge Road of 160 feet – called

The Rope Walk, evidently from there being a rope manufacturers at some time. Part of this was sold – after being arranged into plots – in 1879. 31 plots was sold then averaging about £55 a plot. Later they were all sold at a slight advance, & in 1898 they were sold again – some of them – for £100 a plot. On Plot 1, corner of Stoney Road, was built a shop – or rather two shops on two plots – by a Mr Crispe, who said he invested here especially as he anticipated the Railway would want them. That is true, but he died some years previously. Also here originated the Barking & East Ham Advertiser in 1888 by a Mr J. Mills, a small Printer here[6]. His views was far advanced & exposed many abuses in Barking & also advocated views that is so prominent now in all newspapers. Unfortunately for Mr Mills, his paper [was] too socialistic for that day & it came to grief. He was too poor to stand against the old fashioned dogmatic customs that prevailed in the Town then. The paper – so far as he was concerned – became defunct in 1890. The price was One-Penny.

The Spotted Dog. [Page 458]

I understand there are few signs of the Spotted Dog in Essex. The Gents Magazine says that the sole use of the spotted Dog in this Country is to contribute by its appearance to the splendour of the stable establishment – and also to the carriages - to which he belongs. According to the "Spotted Dog" at Forest-Gate, it must be a very old Sign.

The present house at Barking is a modern structure, but originally the Licence was carried on in one of the Cottages shown in the picture on page [ ] about 60 yards from the present house. It was then kept by Mr Edward Maynard[7], who with his brother James also had a Carmans business. It was about 1870 when he built a house on the site of the present one & the Licence was transferred from the Cottage to the new house. The new house was a plain bricked building with not so many entrances as now. Mr Maynard met

---

6   John Mills, printer, Longbridge Road. (Kelly's 1890).

7   Edward and James Maynard, carriers, Axe Street. (Pigot 1839); Edward Maynard,
     Spotted Dog, East Street. (Kelly's 1871).

with a tragic death in 1878-9 when he was engaged to convey by Brakes[8] a party of School Children – who came from Plaistow by train to Ilford, where in the grounds attached to a large house in the Cranbrook Road, they were to spend a happy day. The Brakes were already at Barking Railway Station, and Mr Maynard- who was very deaf – was crossing the railway (at that time there was the old Kissing gates[9] at this crossing) when a train cut him up to peices. His widow remained in possession for some time afterwards. Mr F. Heathcote[10] later took it, and in 1884 the exterior of the house underwent extensive alterations & altered to the present Elizabethan style. (Mr F. Heathcote & his wife was both much respected. He was a Sportsman & was often seen with his gun going to a shooting match that frequently took place at that time. They had a very large family and after selling the Spotted Dog, he decided to lead a retiring life at Ilford after 17 years in Barking. But he soon decided to go into business again & he took a Public-House at Brentwood. This house was near a Military town, but out of the boundary & unfortunately he was evicted for serving a soldier, who according to Military law should not have been served in this house. He was compelled to sell the house. In August 1904 he - having been Manager of the "Criterion", Margate for about 6 months – eventually decided to purchase it, but he was refused a Licence on account of the said Conviction – which was found out). Also over the Bar [of the Spotted Dog] was altered & converted into a large Concert room 40 feet x 18 feet. In 1895 (March) a fire occurred here through the upsetting of a lamp & did damage to the extent of £100. Also in October 1895 a Burglary occurred here. The thieves stole a silver cup won by the Loyal United Friends at the local Sports & [which] was exhibited here; also 1500 3d Cigars, 6 bottles of Whiskey, 1 Brandy &c, but they were never caught. Mr Heathcote sold the house in the latter part of 1895 to a Mr Emmerson, who still tenants it on behalf of the Railway Company who purchased it when the Bridge was built. Adjoining the house was a small, but pretty, flower garden & in the rear good stables. The two cottages shown in the picture with a large shed or stables attached to each was demolished after the sale in 1891. The following small plan will better explain the Garden and the two old Cottages. The Plan refers to the Sale in 1891. The land is now covered with Bricks & Mortar.

---

8   Break, a horse-drawn wagon.

9   Gates hung in a "U" or "V" shaped enclosure.

10   Frederick Heathcote, Spotted Dog P.H., Longbridge Road. (Kelly's 1890).

From Glenny Road to the Recreation Ground [Page 459] was Agricultural land, farmed by Mr George Augustus Burrell, but in 1898 this land – forming 154 Plots – was sold in June of that year & called the Longbridge Road Estate. On it is two good roads called Faircross & Monteagle Avenues. The same year 137 more Plots was sold which includes Park Avenue. The money realised from these sales was £7582 & £8387 respectively The shop frontages to Longbridge Road realized £5 to £6 per foot frontage.

At the rear of the Above land was another estate sold – called the Harpour Estate – and comprised 131 Plots. It was sold in 1892. On it is 2 Streets viz Harpour Road & Glenny Road (that part continuing from the older road). A large portion of it was resold in 1894 & is now all built upon.

The Recreation Ground.

This extensive & valuable acquisition of so many acres of land for this purpose, reflects credit upon those who was in Authority at Barking in 1895-6. One noble estate after another had been given over to the Builder, & these were situated in the very heart of the Town, & regards position and their historical Associations, either would have suited the purpose admirably.

But as it was too late [Page 460] to acquire any of these Estates, no better situation could have been chosen than the one in Longbridge Road. I beleive the credit is due to the members of the old Local Board, as previous to the adoption of the New Councils Act of 1894, that body did agree to purchase 55 acres of land at £165 an Acre, & 20 acres more was included in the Report to the Local Government Board. As will be seen on another page the New Council elected in 1894 was all new members of a new party formed called the "Progressives" & they soon decided to have a Recreation Ground, the same site as suggested by the old Local Board. This land was good & rich Agricultural land farmed by Mr W. W. Glenny[11], Mr G. A. Burrell[12] & Mr

---

11 William Wallis Glenny, farmer, Cecil House. (Kelly's 1878). An obituary following his death in 1923 reads: " On several branches of agriculture the deceased gentleman was regarded as an authority, particularly on market gardening, and he wrote a good deal on the latter subject. He was formerly Chairman of the Essex Chamber of Agriculture, and was deeply interested in the antiquarian history of the county. Other offices he had held for a time were those of Vice-Chairman of the Kent and Essex Sea Fisheries Committee, and member, and Chairman in 1909, of the Executive Committee of the London Society of East Anglians".

12 George Augustus Burrell. (Kelly's 1871).

Daniel Hawes[13]. From Bamford Place was a narrow lane called "Snakes Lane" only about 100 yards in length, then a stile[14] & from which ran a footpath leading to the Watery Lane. I[t] was a favorite walk. Powers however was obtained to divert this footpath by the Barking & Ilford authorities, as it ran through both parishes. The 20 Acres mentioned was purchased at £200 per Acre & the total number of Acres is 75, but only 9 of these are in Barking Parish. In July 1895 an enquiry was held at the Public Offices for the purpose of considering the proposal of the Council to borrow £15,500 & which was made up as follows. (The Cottages and peice of land now the site of the Royal Oak, although apparently forming a portion of the above land, was not included in the purchase).

Vendors

Sir Edward Hulse. This portion comprises 56 acres	£10,024.0.0
Governors of Christs Hospital 14 acres	£3000.0.0
Cotlands. Trustees of Barking Charities 5 acres	£1000.0.0
Tenants Compensations, Legal & other charges about	£1476.000
Total	**£15500.0.0**

Additional. For excavating the proposed Lake	£1932.0.0
Estimated cost of the Lake	£2271.0.0
Total	**£4203.0.0**

The Lake as originally constructed was 485 yards long & 48 yards wide. The water would come from the natural water course & Loxford Brook. In March 1897 the ground was fenced in at a cost of £283 & the Park being sufficiently ready it was opened to the public on the 9th of April 1897 by Mr C. L. Beard, Chairman of the Council[15]. Also Mr John Bones – head gardener to Mr Mills

---

13 Daniel Hawes, market gardener, Rippleside. (Kelly's 1871).

14 Stile.

15 On page 259 of the manuscript, Frogley writes: "Mr Beard who was elected in the 1894 contest, was in succession to Dr Mason installed as Chairman of the Council. He was foreman at Beckton Gas Works & no doubt illiterate, but he proved himself thoroughly capable as a Chairman. In consequence of holding this position he was for the term of his office a J.P. but I believe he only sat on the Bench once". On page 264 he adds: "He was very successful & respected as Chairman & although a self-educated man he retired honorably in 1898".

of Loxford Hall, & a native of Barking – was appointed Superintendent. In 1898 the Boat house was created at a cost of £59 and in July the same year, Mr Frank Wagstaff[16], another Barking man, secured the contract to supply Boats for the Lake, and also undertook the letting for hire on the Lake. Since 1898 several improvements have taken place here, especially to the Lake, which now undoubtedly ranks with any Lake on or about London.

The Royal Oak [Page 461]

situated at the corner of Longbridge Lane & Waterey Lane[17], and this spot is called "Fair-Cross". The new house was built in 1898 & cost about £2000. It is built on the site of the gardens attached to two Cottages & occupied by a family for many years named Ellmore. Mr Ellmore held a beer licence in one of the cottages[18] but the licence was transferred to the new house, although Mr Ellmore was not the tenant of the latter. Mr Austin Mays, formerly an employee of the Jute Works & later a Newsagent in the Broadway[19] – [moved] from this to the Royal Oak. The house is pleasantly situated & has no doubt proved a very lucrative investment to Mr Mays. From here each lane passes through some lovely rural walks, but probably in a very few years this spot will be robbed of the country aspect it no[w] has.

Manor-Farm[20]. This Farm can be reached from the main road, or by a pathway accross fields commencing opposite the Royal Oak. It was until recent years the residence of some Farmers well known in Barking when Agriculture was a staple industry in Barking. [In] more recent years a Mr Marriott[21] occupied it. He was a successful Electrical Engineer of London, but he took great interest in all Local Matters. He was elected to the Council in 1894 & was its Chairman in 1898. Singularly although a staunch

---

16 Harry Wagstaff, 11 Cambridge Road; John Wagstaff, 63 Westbury Road. (Kelly's 1895).

17 Now South Park Drive.

18 John Elmore, beer retailer, Faircross. (Kelly's 1862). Elmore family in: East of London Family History Society *1851 census index series: vol.1, part 4*. 1984. p.12.

19 Austin Mays, stationer, Broadway. (Kelly's 1890).

20 Manor Farm, earlier called Jenkins Farm, was built in the late 18th century on the site of Jenkins manor house. It was demolished in 1937. The site is now in Mayesbrook Park.

21 William Kenez Mariott, Manor House, Longbridge Road. (Kelly's 1902). He was chairman of the Barking and Ripple Conservative Association for many years.

Conservative he was in Local Matters in dead sympathy & an active member of the Progressive & Socialistic parties, but in general Politics the reverse. He was succeeded by a Mr Patterson, who so very recently has figured prominently as Defendant in Criminal Proceedings, but I do not think anything that would stain his reputation. It was a financial transaction. The house is moderately large, built of ordinary brick & of modern structure. It lays some distance from the main road surrounded by beautiful meadows & orchards. One old family of farmers who held this Farm was the "Biggs"[22]– also the "Meads".

Longbridge Farm[23] – no doubt from which the road is named after, but some say after a Brook of that name. This picturesque house is close to Jenkins and which dated back to the "Fanshawe time" was demolished in 1860, and evidently the present Farm-house built on its site. For many years & until his death Mr John Pickering Peacock[24], a fine built & splendid specimen of an Old English Farmer & Gentleman [lived here]. (The Manor of Woodgrange, Forest Gate, was sold to John Pickering Esqr, & in 1814 a relative name[d] John Pickering Peacock was in possession. The latter however afterwards resided at Whalebone House, Chadwell-Heath[25]. What this Mr Peacock was previous to marrying into the Pickering family I do not know, but when he resided at Whalebone House he kept a Private School there & in 1900 I saw the old bell on the top of the house as was often to be seen in those days. He was also a Churchwarden of Dagenham Church, but in 1827 the Rev T. L. Fanshawe, Vicar, declined to accept him as his Warden, but chose Mr Pollett of East-bury House[26]. Mr Pollett died in 1844. This Mr Peacock was the

---

22   Edwin Biggs, farmer, Bennett's Castle; George Biggs, farmer, Longbridge; James Biggs, farmer. (White's 1848). James Biggs, farmer, Manor Farm. (Pigot 1839, Kelly's 1851). Mrs Charlotte Biggs, farmer, East Street. (Kelly's 1871).

23   In its later years, Longbridge Farm was known as Brown's Farm, after the tenant, Robert George Brown (1852-1932), who also farmed Goodmayes Farm on the other side of Longbridge Road. His father and eventually his son farmed at Gaysham Hall, Barkingside, where the family are buried in Holy Trinity churchyard.

24   John Pickering Peacock, farmer, Longbridge. (Kelly's 1851, 1871). The 1851 census shows John Pickering Peacock of Longbridge Farm, aged 26, to have been born in Dagenham, and one can deduce that his wife Charlotte was a Higgs. Surveyor, Ripple, 1855, 1865-6; Churchwarden, 1854-8, 1867. *Barking vestry minutes.* 1955. p.323.

25   Jno. Pickering Peacock, Whalebone House. (Pigot 1839).

26   George Pollett, farmer, Eastbury House. (White's 1848).

Frogley's drawing of Westbury House in 1800. Page 224 in the manuscript. (See pages 32 - 35).

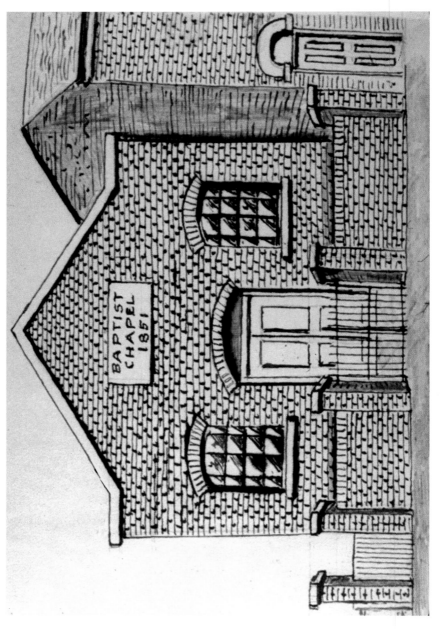

Page 279 in the manuscript. (See page 154).

44 Longbridge Road in 1980.

Coloured postcard of the boating lake in Barking Park.

20

A photograph of Father Benfield from page 292 in the manuscript. (See page 139)

— AN OLD VIEW IN THE BROADWAY — *From Lysons. DATE 1803* —

Page 61 in the manuscript.

See page 39.

The view of Dagenham Beach (Breach?) House referred to on page 507 of the manuscript. (See page 160).

father of Mr J. P. Peacock of Longbridge Farm, Mr Peacock died in 1878 & [is] buried in Barking Church Yard). It was always said, and I beleive it was true, that rarely was a weary traveller or tramp turned away without receiving some hospitality if they had the courage to apply for it. Late in the 18th century the Skinner family resided there[27], and in 1778 Ambrose Skinner died there & his wife Ann in 1789. The "Skinners" was a wealthy family & some of them also held & resided at Aldersbrooke. [This] being the terminus of Longbridge Road I will now come back to Fair-Cross-Farm, situated opposite the Recreation Ground.

Fair-Cross-Farm[28] **[Page 462]**

Fair Cross Farm is bounded by the Longbridge Road & Upney-Lane, & contains about 47 Acres of rich & fertile land. It contains a neat but small farm-house with good stables, Barns & the usual outbuildings. A Mr Plows[29], who lived at Braintree House in North Street & [was] a Smackowner, by selling his vessels purchased this farm, but sold it, & left Barking for Australia in 1849. Then I am informed Mr Thomas Patch[30] became possessed of it. He was a native of Barking & by his energy & perseverance raised himself from a humble position to one of comparative affluence. He also filled various [positions] on he Local Authority. In 1876 the freehold of this

---

27 From the late 17th to the early 19th century, there were at least four generations of Skinners at Longbridge, where the eldest was called Ambrose. Longbridge Farm was the site on 19th December 1734 of a daring raid made by Dick Turpin and the Gregory Gang, when Ambrose Skinner, the tenant, and members of his household were tied up at gunpoint and the house ransacked. Derek Barlow: *Dick Turpin and the Gregory Gang.* 1972. p.51-56.

28 Faircross is an ancient place-name and probably commemorates the home of Cecily, widow of Hugh de Cruce. Known as Fairecrouch in 1456 and Ffayercrosse in 1609. *Place-names of Essex.* 1935. p.90,

29 Thomas Plows, smack owner, North Street. (Pigot 1839); farmer. (White's 1848).

30 See East of London Family History Society *1851 census index series: vol.1:part 4: Essex: Barking.* 1984. p.26, for Patch family. In the 1861 census Thomas Patch, aged 53, is listed as a farmer of 69 acres employing 12 men, 4 boys and 6 women. According to Pat Bass, he must be the brother of her great-great-grandfather John Patch who was christened on the same day as another brother William in 1814 at St Margaret's, Barking. They were the sons of Thomas (a fisherman) and Mary Patch. In the 1861 census John, aged 48, is an agricultural labourer living at 6 Railway Cottage, and William, aged 45, is a market gardener. Their sister Sarah was christened at St Margaret's in 1818 and died in Elham in 1888, aged 73.

Farm – including all buildings – was offered for sale & Mr Thomas Patch was the tenant at a Rental of £234 per Annum. In 1879 the Royal Agricultural Society offered prizes for the best managed Market Garden Farms & Mr Patch obtained 2nd prize in Class II. He died here 12 Feb 188-, Aged 70 & his widow carried on the Farm[31]. She died March 1897, Age 82. Shortly after her husbands death her nephew – Mr Watkins – managed the Farm for her but he was not so successful. In Oct 1899 the whole of the horses, carts and implements was sold by auction, and about a year afterwards Mr C. Goodman took it over[32]. Mr Goodman also had a Farm at Greengate Street Plaistow on a portion of which is built the Tramway Stables &c. Mr Goodman represented Ripple Ward[33] on the Local Board & District Council. He died in September 1907.

I have already stated that this road - a few years ago a country lane [Page 464] – has undergone many changes. In April 1888 the Local Surveyor, Mr C. J. Dawson[34], submitted plans & suggestions for the intended improvements in this Road, as there was every appearance of this being the chief residential part of the Town. A great many residences had already been erected & the owners subscribed to a fund to provide trees along the road. In Nov 1888, 23 trees was planted & the Local Board immediately took over the care of them & protected them with wooden guards. Also 4 lamps were erected to light this portion adjacent to the Spotted Dog. It must be noted that all the houses was erected on the right hand side from the station & a hedge mostly still remained, but in 1889 the owners sold to the Local Board a few feet of their

31 Mrs Patch, Tunbridge House, Longbridge Road. (Kelly's 1890); 52 Longbridge Road. (Kelly's 1895).

32 Charles Goodman, Faircross Farm. (Kelly's 1890).

33 One of the four divisions of the ancient parish of Barking.

34 On page 253 of the manuscript, Frogley writes: "Mr Charles Dawson, Surveyor, of Cambridge Rd Barking. His salary then [1883] was £80 per annum, and he was not required to give his whole time to the Board. Both the father & Grandfather of Mr C. Dawson had been Surveyors in the town, & Mr C. Dawson received his experience from a large & noted London firm. In addition to his salary there was a certain percentage upon all undertakings by the Board, thus in consequence of the costly improvements that took place yearly, his appointment rapidly advanced him". On page 261, he adds: "March 1896. Mr C. Dawson junr appointed Assistant Surveyor – under his father – at a Salary of £90 per Annum. Later in the year Mr C. J. Dawson Senr Resigned & his son was appointed Surveyor. Mr C. J. Dawson Senr was retained as a consulting Engineer & his fee to be £50 a year".

frontage to widen the road. This purchase cost £150. In May 1889 this portion of the Road was sewered at a cost of £115 & the cost of tar-paving & kerbing to Fair-Cross Farm cost £567. New fence on the opposite side (left) cost £45. In 1896 from the Railway Crossing to Faircross Farm lamps was placed or erected for the first time. The number of houses (& shops) demolished in 1906 & 7 on the right hand side was 15 & for which the owners was well compensated[35]. A cottage still standing & used as an office for the Railway Co was sold by the owner for £690. This house was the home of the writer[36]. Adjoining is some small modern houses belonging to a Mr J. Smith, Contractor &c[37] & he sold the forecourts only for £600 to the Council I believe as their Tramway Service was to be extended from the Ripple Road corner of East Street to the Loxford Bridge to met the Ilford Section. Adjoining Mr Smith's houses is another belonging to a Mr Wilson[38], the Forecourt of which was also sold for £140 (more than all the ground cost originally).

Wakering Road[39]. One side of this road was demolished for the railway Extension in 1906-7. The road was made in 1871-2 & building soon commenced. By 1873 the whole of the land in this road was sold. One Cottage – Crown Cottage – in this road was built by a Mr John Howe, late of the Hop-Pole Fisher Street (now closed)[40]. The story runs that Mrs Howe

---

35 Between April and June 1905, Barking Council built a tramway line along Longbridge Road and Fanshawe Avenue to connect with Ilford tramways at Loxford Bridge. Until mid-1907 the level crossing at Barking station prevented connection to their line along East Street, so they leased the stretch from Loxford to the Ilford Council tramways until the road bridge had been built to replace the level crossing.

36 Windsor Cottage, 44 Longbridge Road.

37 John Smith, builder, Wishford House, Longbridge Road. (Kelly's 1890).

38 John Wilson, J.P., 62 Longbridge Road. (Kelly's 1920).

39 Wakering Road, like its neighbour, must have owed its name to the Glenny family. Before the 1870s, their residence – Cecil House in East Street – had been called Cobb or Cobblers Hall, which had been built near the site of a large late Tudor house first called Wakering Place and then Cobblers Hall, before being pulled down in the late 17th century (it is shown on the map of Barking manor of 1652-3). The Glennys were aware of the earlier name because it was in their title deeds. The name Wakering certainly went back further than Wakering Place because fields north of East Street were called Great and Little Wakerings in the Middle Ages. The connection made by Reaney in *Place-names of Essex* - "Probably so called from the family of Ida de Wakering (1254) " - is probably supposititious.

40 John Howe, 12 Wakering Road. (Kelly's 1895).

had a mania for saving all the Crown-Peices she became possessed of, unknown to her husband, until the house was sold, whe[n] she confessed the fact. The floor was taken up (where she hid them) & there was such a number that out of that hoard they built a house (in 1874) in Wakering Road & called it "Crown Cottage", as also a stone on the front of the house announced it. I am told the house was demolished in 1906-7 for the Railway extension. The first houses (villas) erected in this road still stands. The age of Glenny Road is about the same as Wakering Road.

Ripple-Road. [Pages 401-418]

This road is probably the most ancient of the main roads that lead to the town, & no doubt when so many Feudal Lords resided in the Parish century after century, the nobility that travelled this road so frequently made it in that day the most important. One family alone, out of scores of others, viz the Fanshawe family, is sufficient to make this both interesting & notorious, but for nearly a hundred years after these great City Merchants ceased to reside here, the road assumed an aspect of a quiet country lane & continued in this state until about 1880 [when] the local authorities began their so called improvements, which means that for the future it will have an industrial aspect & the residents of the working class. This road commences from East-Street & passing Axe Street proceeds to Rippleside, Rainham &c. Commencing from East Street on the right is the Paddock (noticed under East Street) and on the left is the Vicarage Grounds & Vicarage, for many years noted for the various fetes & shows held by the local Societies. (For the vicarage see "The Church"). This portion of the road extending from East Street to Axe Street, was always known as "The Island" & still is by the Old inhabitants. This portion in 1889 was widened & lighted at a cost of about £2500. That sum was raised for the purpose – the loan to extend over 20 years. I must mention this "improvement" to this road was discussed for some years – several of the Ground Landlords gave their frontages – or strips – for the purpose while others received a nominal sum & the above loan. At a later period (1908) a strip of land off the Paddock was purchased by the Council from Mr T. W. Glenny. The Vicarage ground was also deprived of a strip to widen the road in 18--[41] and the consideration was that the Council

---

41   The last two digits of the date have been obliterated.

build a new substantial Brick-wall. Next is Hawthorne Terrace. This small terrace was built in 1873[42] by Mr Hawes, farmer of Barking & dying about 1878 his widow eventually married Mr. Chalk, Stationmaster at Barking (L.T. & S. Ry)[43]. (Mr Daniel Hawes, previous to building Hawthorn Terrace, resided in Queens Road for many years & was noted for his splendid flower gardens. The land adjoining his residence extended to the water tower & was then an Orchard. It is now built on. There was only 3 houses on that side of Queens Road then, viz Roden lodge – the said orchard - & two houses at the other end). Mr Chalk received £120 in 1892 for a strip of the frontage of the terrace & a field adjoining called "Chalk Barn Field", a peice of land that formerly [was] part of a field that contained 5 Acres & was sold in 1799 to Mrs Deborah Glenny for £1800, having previous to that been let on a lease at a yearly rental of £54.

The new Police Station built in ----[44]. The old Police Station is noticed under North Street. The Justice Court was originally at Ilford & held at the "Angel" Inn. An order or Authority to keep a Justice Court at Ilford was granted in July 1558 & was addressed to Sir Edward Waldegrave "To keep the above Court in the absence of the Earl of Sussex, Chief Justice of all Forests south of the Trent & during his stay as Lord Deputy of Ireland".

The Horse Pond was on the opposite side of the road to the present St Pauls Church. As seen by my rough sketch a black fence divided the pond into two Parts – one side on the meadow portion & the other used by Carters. Another strong white wooden fence divided the pond from the roadway. In the improvements [already] spoken of the pond was filled up & the whole made level with the road. Curiously before doing this the ownership of the pond was disputed. The Lord of the Manor however claimed it & in April 1890 his Steward wrote to the Local Board offering the site for £100. The Board however, considering the number of years the Public had the free use of it, repudiated the claims and eventually filled it up. The site of the pond is Nos 100-104 Ripple Road & land adjoining.

---

42 Possibly earlier. Kelly's 1871 lists Mrs Baines, Walter Buckell, James Moffat and Mrs Plunkett at Hawthorn Terrace, Rippleside.

43 London, Tilbury & Southend Railway.

44 1910. *Barking and Dagenham buildings past and present.* 1992. p.59.

St Pauls Church[45]. The site of this Church – given by the late Marquis of Salisbury – was known as the Berry-Barn-Field[46], as a large wooden & thatched Barn occupied the site. In 1874 this Barn was fully stored with wheat ready to be thrashed, but some young children playing in it with matches the Barn & wheat was totaly destroyed by the fires & waters[47]. The Local Firemen was there & depended upon water from the Horsepond, but their Hose would not reach the Barn. From the Barn to Ripple Road was some Allotments, let to men in the employ of Mr W. W. Glenny. In April 1892 a Church Committee met in a room at Fenchurch Street Station, when the Tenders being opened, Mr Parmenter of Braintree, Essex was accepted. It was decided to build the Church in two portions – the first consisted of the Chancel & two Bays o the Nave at a cost of £3890 of which the following sums had been raised, viz:- From the Bishop of St Albans Trust £1500: Incorporated Church Building Society £200: Essex Churches £50: and Private Donation £2044 – Total £3794.0.0. The Memorial Stone was laid by the Marchioness of Waterford on 9th June 1892. The following account of this Church appeared at the time:-

It will be erected from designs of Sir Arthur Blomfield & Sons & which are in the late Perpendicular style, & estimated to accommodate 890 persons including a Choir of [?][48]. To consist of a Nave 86 feet x 25 feet, Chancel 35 feet x 25 feet, Ailes[49] 86 feet x 15 feet 9 inches. A South Chapel 31 feet 9 inches x 18 feet 6 inches & on the North side an Organ Chamber. Vestries: the Choir Vestry over that intended for the Clergy & which will be reached by a Turret-Staircase from a Porch on the North side. The walls above the brick footings to consist of an outside casing of broken flint with quoins &c of red brick – an inner casing of red brick built in alternate courses of beading & stretchers. The spaces between these courses being filled in with a course of Portland Cement Concrete. The columns of the Nave Arcades to

---

45   The Church was destroyed by enemy action on 14th January 1945. *On the home front: Barking and Dagenham in World War II*. 1990. p.70.

46   Berry Barn was Westbury Barn and was probably the medieval tithe barn attached to Westbury manor. Aaron Bowles is listed in 1890 as foreman to W. W. Glenny at Burybarn Farm, Ripple Road.

47   According to the *Essex Times* (30 August 1873), this fire actually took place on the afternoon of 25th August 1873 and "resulted in total destruction".

48   The handwriting is not very clear here – it might read "30".

49   Aisles.

be of red purpose made bricks. All the external Wrought Stone work including the windows, as also the Caps & Bases of the Columns of the Nave Arcades, will be in Bath Stone. The other internal stone work to be in Corsham Stone. The floors with the exception of the Chancel, Sanctuary &c - which will be tiled – are to be laid with wooden blocks. The open timber roofs will be constructed of Fir & that of the Nave being covered with Tiles & the Aisles, South Chapel &c with lead. Clerestory windows to be placed over each Bay of the Nave Arcade, also windows of the same description & a large East window will light the Chancel. The entrance will consist of a large central western door & doors at the North-West & South-West corners of the Aisles. A bell to be hung in the Turret placed at the western end, & the total cost of the whole building as per tender accepted £6514. At the opening ceremony in ---- £50 was collected.

It has been noticed that this road was widened a considerable distance & among others who sold strips of their frontages was W. W. Glenny Esqr for £50: Mr Mills £30: & Mr Brown £3 – these strips was in that portion from Westbury Road to Upney Lane. Another strip was situated opposite the Westbury Arms & [was] sold by the Owner, Mr Yeoman[50] – an ex-Police Constable at Barking – for £150 to the Local Board.

St Margarets Estate. This estate comprised a fine large meadow and is shown in the sketch at the rear of the Horse-Pond. It extended from the Ripple Road to Byfrons Park (see Axe Street) & was known as the Park – mostly Glennys Park. It was a good grazing field & many local fetes was held on it. It contained nearly 18 acres. Thomas Glenny[51] who died in 1861 possessed it & he left it by Will to his wife Harriett (in Trust) during her life time. She died 24th Feby 1876 & [was] buried at the Ilford Cemetery. With the exception of a strip of this estate – facing Axe Street – the whole was sold in Nov 1876 to Sir Willoughby Smith[52] for £3890 & this was again sold in 1881 – with West-bury (opposite) – to the British Land Company, who planned & laid the whole out for Building purposes. This Estate was cut up into about 365 Plots, but in consequence of the other Estates adjoining also being sold & built upon it is difficult to define where one begin[s] & the other ends, but as will be seen from the Plan on the next page, this Estate

---

50   Alfred Yeoman, Linton Road. (Kelly's 1890).

51   Thomas Glenny, farmer & market gardener, Bull Street. (Kelly's 1851).

52   Willoughby Smith, Westbury House. (Kelly's 1878).

comprises some 5 roads & their total length is about 3876 feet. They were kerbed, carriage way rolled, sewered & made up at a cost of £2500 & in 1888 35 lamps were erected & later the whole estate lighted.

[13 plots sold to Mr Copeland]. This strip formed a portion of this Estate & was included in the sale of 1876 & was sold again in 1878 to Mr Copeland, a retired Tallyman, for £1760. He later sold to the Local Board (Marked in the annexed plan 6 foot passage) a large plot for a roadway from Axe Street to St Anns Road, which in 1889 cost the Board £126 to make up. In Plots 11, 12 & 13 was two old wooden cottages & a Blacksmiths shop – occupied by a Mr Cannon[53]. They were almost hid by the numbers of Trees that surrounded them & a rustic hedge. It was a picturesque corner & all was cleared away in 1878.

The Stag, [Page 408]

A small Beer-House at the corner of St Anns Road, was first opened as an off-Licence in 1883, and in 1884 an on-Licence was obtained, during the tenancy of Mr William Collier, formerly of Vine Cottage, Tanner Street. He now (1898) resides at Southend.

The Westbury-House Estate. (Westbury House [is] so named no doubt from its position being West of Eastbury-House). This Estate, or Manor Farm, was a parcel of the possessions of Barking-Abbey & originally was an extensive Estate. In – or after – the Dissolution it became the property of Henry VIII who granted it in 1545 to Sir William Denham. (Sir William Denham, born at Leystone, Devonshire, became M.P. & sheriff of London in 1541 & about this time he was knighted. About 1544-5 he being a favorite received from the Crown a grant of 13 Manors & amongst which was East-bury: Stonehall & Gayshams: & Westbury all in Barking Parish & some other lands also). In this Grant went with Westbury 1000 acres of Arable land: 600 of pasture: 100 of Meadow: 80 of Wood & 500 of Furze & Heath, a very extensive estate. Sir William Denham died 4th August 1548, when it went to William Abbot and who sold it to Clement Sisley[54], Gent, in 1557. (William Abbot of Hartland, was son of William Abbot, Serjeant to the cellar of King Henry

---

53   James Cannon, blacksmith, Axe Street. (Kelly's 1871).

54   On page 408 Frogley includes a footnote regarding the Sisley (Sysley) family, which is omitted here.

VIII. He married Mariera[55], daughter of Sir William Denham, & at the death of the latter inherited his Estates).

The next possessor [of Westbury] was Edward Breame Esqr[56] & he died in 1560, but his descendants evidently possessed it, as Arthur Breame Esqr sold it to Thomas Fanshawe in 1574[57] and [it] passed from them to Blackbourn Poulton Esqr[58], but the tenant at Westbury at this time was Mr Richard Meadows – who died there in 1679. In 1700 Blackbourn Poulton was in possession & his son – Blackbourn Poulton - Attorney at Law – sold his Reversion in this [Page 410]

Estate to Sir Crispe Gascoyne in 1745. I notice from my searches that at the death of Blackbourn Poulton Senr this Estate was held by his son Poulton Allen (Alleyne) and after his death reverted to Blackbourn Poulton Junr – who, as stated, sold his Reversion to Sir Crispe Gascoyne. The Alleyne family (sometimes spelled Allen) evidently enjoyed the influence of Sir Crispe. They resided at Westbury House & also possessed the Dove-House-Estate in Barking. Probably Poulton through marriage assumed the name of Allen. A descendant, Ann, wife of Poulton Allen, died in 1807. She was a daughter of John Cocking Esqr, Surgeon of Barking. Mr Thomas Alleyne or Allen in 1750 held the Dove-House-Estate & another of this family, The Rev Robert Allen, was Chaplain to Ilford Hospital in 1786, but he resided at Islington[59]. Many of this family is buried in Barking Churchyard. Blackbourn

---

55   Should be Margery.

56   Footnote by Frogley: The Breame family appears to have been seated at East-Ham & was very wealthy. Richard Breame in 1544 was granted the great Tithes of East-Ham, including the Rectory & Ad[v]owsons of East-Ham Church by Henry VIII. He died June 1546 and was succeeded by Edward Breame who died in 1558-60. There was a "Brass" in East Ham Church in Memory of Margaret Breame who died [in] 1558 & [was the] wife of Richard. The Brass was seen[?] in 1719 but I am informed it has gone now. Arthur Breame, brother of Edward, succeeded & he married Anne daughter of Robert Allingham Esqr of Cambridge. He was succeeded by Giles Breame, son & heir of Arthur. This Giles gave the Almshouses to the Poor of East-Ham. He died [in] 1621 possessed of East-Ham Manor. There is a Monument to his Memory in the Chancel of East-Ham Old Church.

57   Footnote inserted by Frogley at this point: John Jones[?], Gent, died at Westbury, Barking, in 1592.

58   Blackburn Poulton, Churchwarden, Ripple, 1695; Churchwarden, Chadwell, 1696. *Barking vestry minutes*. 1955. p. 324.

59   Frogley was right about Allen's residence in Islington, but Bert Lockwood wonders where he got his information. The Revd Bennet Allen came from a Hertfordshire family. See his: *The Revd Bennet Allen: chaplain extraordinary*. 2001. *passim*.

Poulton Junr died in 1749, but two years previous Sir Crispe Gascoyne sold a portion of this Estate – including Westbury House – to Joseph Keeling Esqr[60]. Mr Keeling in addition to Westbury, also possessed the Abbey site, Cricklewood & Perrymans Farms. Cricklewood was situated near Seven-Kings, Ilford & Perrymans at Barking-side, at the rear of the "Horns" Inn, & the small Farm House – called Abbey Lodge – still stands.

Mr Keeling was a Collector of Customs, and was married first to Hester – widow of Mr Plomer of Hoddesdon, Herts & daughter of Marmaduke Rawdon of Hoddesdon, a Gent – who possessed a Manor in Winistree to which she succeeded and conveyed it to Joseph Keeling in 1751. She died in 1756 without issue. His second wife was Alice Slaney – widow of Joseph Slaney Esqr - & by whom [he] had four children: Joseph, John, William & Mary. Joseph Keeling in 1766 was High Sheriff of Essex & he died in 1792 & [was] buried in the Churchyard. His Widow, at his death, succeeded to his Estates. She died in 1828 aged 92, & their eldest son Joseph Keeling succeeded her. Westbury House & grounds was later possessed by Mr John Scrafton Thompson, of Clements House, Ilford[61], the House being tenanted by Mr Crow. Mr Thompson in 1843 sold Westbury to Dr John Manley[62]. Dr Manley previously resided in the White House, East Street & he married a daughter of John Lambert Esqr, Farmer, Broadway, Barking. He appears to have had a very successful practice here & held several local positions in the town. He was a Churchwarden, Charities Trustee &c &c. He sold – in 1876 – Westbury & left the town for Teddington, Middlesex where he died in May 1877, & [was] buried in his wifes tomb in Barking Churchyard. His wife Ann died in June 1870. The purchaser in 1876 was Sir Willoughby Smith, Electrical Engineer of 44 New North Road, London[63]. In 1883 he was elected

---

60   Joseph Keeling, Surveyor, 1750-1. *Barking vestry minutes*. 1955. p.322.

61   John Scrafton Thompson, Ilford. (Pigot 1839).

62   John Manley, Medical Officer, 1834-6; Churchwarden, 1843-58. *Barking vestry minutes*. 1955. p.322. John Manley, MD, Bull Street. (Pigot 1839).

63   Willoughby Smith (1828-1891) was chief electrician of the Telegraph Construction Company, assisting on the Great Eastern with re-laying the transatlantic cable, and then taking charge of the French Atlantic cable expedition. He wrote *The progress of submarine telegraphy* in 1891. He did experimental work on insulating and conducting materials, and later in wireless telegraphy and telephony. Around 1873, he discovered "that light would lower the electrical resistance of a selenium rod. This, the photoelectric effect, is the basis of all facsimile and television systems". However, Frogley seems to be mistaken in attributing Smith with a knighthood, despite his contribution to electronic engineering.

to the high office of President of the Society of Telegraphic & Electrical Engineers. Sir W. Smith also in 1876 purchased the Park opposite & he sold the two Estates in 1880-1 to the British Land Company for £7050, as he decided to leave the Town. The Company later formed roads on both estates & sold – in plots – and by about 1884 I beleive the whole was disposed of. When Sir Willoughby Smith left the town, it was felt by all that the town received a great loss – He & his family was so respected.

The following **[Page 411]**

is a description of the House (Westbury) as given at the time of sale. The House was plainly built of red brick, and from its appearance I should say it was quite 200 years old or older. Wether a larger house ever stood here I cannot say, but Westbury was not large. It contained on the upper floor 6 bedrooms: on the first floor was 4 bedrooms, study & dressing rooms: on the ground floor was the entrance & inner halls with pannelled walls: Drawing room 28 feet by 14 feet 9 inches with French casements opening to a good garden & Conservatory, also the Dining Room with pannelled walls 19 feet 6 inches x 14 feet 9 inches: large Breakfast room: Butlers-pantry, Bathroom, Kitchen, &c. Adjoining the House was a well kept garden & paddocks & which had a frontage to the Ripple Road of about 100 feet & 360 feet deep containing 3 Rods 13 poles. Also adjoining on the South-side was an ornamental ground [of] 2 Rods 13 poles & having a frontage to Ripple Road of 130 feet & 140 feet deep. This fine old historical House, was doomed & demolished and a road formed – called now Westbury – with a bend in it so that at each end is the Ripple road (see plan). Westbury Road encloses the House & gardens. In 1895 this road was made up at a cost of £414.

Westbury Arms. This modern built house is on the Corner of Ripple Road and King Edwards Road. On its site was originally a licenced house called the "Hand and Bowl", but more recently the house was occupied by Mr Thomas Holland, farmer[64], and attached was the usual out-buildings, Barns &c. King Edwards Road was then a narrow lane – called Hollands Lane - & [was also known as] Hand & Bowl lane. Mr Holland died in 1893. Attached to the farming business Mr Holland created a Milk business, about the only one at that time that carried Milk around the town. His son William Holland succeeded [and] also obtained a beer licence which however he sold in 1897

---

64   Thomas Holland, cowkeeper. (White's 1848, Kelly's 1851); Thomas and William Holland, market gardeners, Rippleside. (Kelly's 1871).

& leaving the town took the Prince Albert at Bexley, Kent. The Present Westbury Arms was built in 1899 – having I was informed had a full provisional Licence granted to the purchaser – Mr Lindsay – some surrenders being made for the purpose & one was the "Rose" in East Street. Mr Lindsay was formerly a ships carpenter, but he married Mrs Saga, widow, of the Libra Arms, Stratford Road, Plaistow & which he sold in 1896. From Mr Lindsay it was purchased by Mr Martin[65].

Gascoigne Estate. [Page 412]

This Estate extends from the Ripple Road & to the rear of the Westbury Arms. It was the property of Mr Edward Glenny of Byfrons[66], but at his death his estates went to his sons Edward & Samuel – one portion called "Gascoigne" belonged to Edward & the other portion called Melborne to Samuel. In Mar 1889, Gascoigne Estate having been cut up into plots was sold.

Melborne Estate, probably so named after the Australian city, where Mr Samuel Glenny had resided[67], was also cut up for building purposes. It extended to the Jute Factory & Fisher Street & the roads on it is Boundary, Gascoigne & Bamber [Roads]. The first sale of plots on this estate was in June 1890 – the prices averaging £23 a plot. Gascoigne Road in 1895 was made up & sewered at a cost of about £260.

Movers Lane. This lane leads also to Creeks-mouth. Down this lane is a small but delapidated farm house, now used as a dairy. Once a good family resided in this house named "Cuff"[68], & they possessed other lands in the

---

65   The purchaser of the Westbury Arms, of whose identity Frogley seems uncertain, was Mr (later Colonel) Albert Edward Martin, who also opened the Electric Cinema in Ripple Road in 1910. Martin was elected to the Barking Urban District Council for South Ward in 1902. He became Liberal MP for Romford South constituency in the post-war election of 1918, and was Barking's first Charter Mayor in 1931.

66   Edward Glenny, market gardener, Bifrons House, Axe Street. (Kelly's 1871).

67   According to one obituary, "Twelve of his early years were spent in Victoria, Australia, where he joined the artillery when "troops" were withdrawn, and "batteries" substituted by the Rt. Hon. W. E. Gladstone in 1879. He collaborated with the Hon. James Munro, Minister of Education, and later served under the Hon. J. Byrne and the Hon. James Paterson, Prime Minister of Victoria. Returning to England in 1881, he settled in Barking, and took a prominent part in public life".

68   There is a memorial on the outer north aisle at St Margaret's Church, Barking, to: "Mary Allen Cuff, wife of Joseph Cuff Esq of Movers...d.1807 [aged] 50; Also of the aforesaid Joseph Cuff...d.1817 [aged] 64; Also of Mr Joseph Cuff, Son of the above...d.1836 [aged] 53".

Town. Joseph Cuff of Whitechapel resided in this house & dying in 1817 was buried at Barking[69]. In 1805 he purchased Brick House Farm, Leigh, Essex, with 150 acres of land for £3800. His eldest son Joseph, of Ash, Kent, succeeded his father, but according to his fathers will the Leigh property went to Thomas –[the] youngest son. Thomas married a Mary Adams & after assumed the name of Cuff Adams & selling the Leigh Property in 1864 went to reside at Bath (History of Rochford[70]). A descendant, Henry David Cuff, of Whitechapel, died Nov 1884 & his wife 1872. Both [are] buried in Little Ilford Churchyard.

Kennedy Estate, was formerly Copyhold, but it was converted into Freehold by the owner in 1857. This land was offered for sale in 1886, but it proved very unsaleable & I believe it was not until Sept 1890 that the last 83 plots was sold. There was also a difficulty in draining & sewering this Estate but in May 1897 a scheme was arrived at – the estimated cost of which was over £5000[71]. The roads on this Estate is:- Movers: Kennedy: Devons: St Johns: Sparshott & Gordon Roads.

Eldred Road. This small thoroughfare adjoins the level crossing & was formerly the property of the Railway Company. In 1893 it contained only a few houses, some of which was sold in July 1893 together with a peice of land sufficient to build about 60 cottages. From this road in 1896 (January) Ripple Road was lighted up to the Harrow Inn.

---

69 This Joseph Cuff (1753-1817) lived at Movers, the site of which is now incorporated into Greatfields Park. He retired to Bath after his wife's death in 1807. His father was Jacob Cuff (1723-1762), the son of Joseph Cuff, farmer, of Winterbourne Whitechurch, Dorset. Jacob was described as a victualler in 1744 when he was made a freeman of the Glovers Company by redemption. He had four children – Sarah, John, William and Joseph. The latter was apprenticed to William Knight, a grocer of Barking, in 1768, and went on to become Junior Warden of the Drapers Company in 1803. He was established as a cheesemonger in Whitechapel from 1780. His youngest son Thomas (1796-1874) married Mary Adams and the family name was changed to Adams by deed poll in 1842, reverting by custom subsequently to Cuffe-Adams. (Information from correspondence between E. J. Cuffe-Adams and James Howson (20 September 1965)).

70 Philip Benton: *The history of Rochford Hundred*. 3 vols. 1867-1888.

71 The most serious problems with "bad ground and the excessive ... subsoil water" were experienced in about 1900 when laying drains in the section of Kennedy Road now renamed Harrow Road, which ran parallel to the West Mayesbrook stream. Steam pumps had to work day and night to clear the water, and costs ran well over estimate. Barking Urban District Council: *Sanitary Committee minutes*. 7th January 1900.

The Harrow – a Beer House on the left hand side of Ripple Road. The name of this house is taken from "Agriculture". The Licence was obtained in 1815 by Stephen Sawkins[72] – an old family of Rippleside. He held it for 40 years. The next owner was Mr James Poole[73] who died in 1894 – having held the Licence also for 40 years & the house is still in this family. Attached to the house is about 2 Acres of land & 200 fruit trees, but when in [ ] the New Branch of Railway line from Barking to Pitsea was constructed, the Company purchased from Mr Poole a strip of this land at a good price. Mr Poole was known to theboys & girls there as "Bogey Poole". [Page 413]

He was also a Market gardener, but the house some 30 years ago was well known for its small annual fair, where the Greasy Pole was notorious. This was discontinued about 1874. From here this road still retains some of its rustic appearance, but the traffic is greater.

Thatched House. This Inn is nearer to East-bury House, and as the name denotes, the old house had a heavy thatched roof & has belonged to Mr Thomas Glenny of Barking, Brewer, for many years[74]. The old house was plastered & whitewashed & when the surrounding land was used for agriculture it was conspicious for long distances – the writer has often seen it from the Ilford Lane. The Bar was only a small room & the tap-room – although low pitched – had a fine view of Eastbury Level. It had a door in the centre with a Bay window sash & contained 6 rooms. Attached was 7

---

72   Stephen Sawkins, beerhouse, Ripple Ward. (White's 1848); beer retailer, Rippleward. (Kelly's 1851). Nineteen Sawkins are listed in the 1851 census.

73   James Pool, beer retailer, Rippleside. (Kelly's 1871, 1878, 1890).

74   It was customary for farmers to brew their own beer to supply the workers in the fields with refreshment at harvesting time and on other special occasions. Barking Brewery was started by Dr George Glenny in 1864 to meet the demands of a few local farmers who had neither the plant nor the necessary skill to produce satisfactory beer themselves. The first brew was made in the potato shed of William Wallis Glenny and, apart from farm consumption, the first cask of beer was purchased by Dr Galloway of Cambridge Road, Barking. George Glenny sold the business to his brother, Thomas W. Glenny (d.1914), who acquired a site on the east side of Linton Road and built the Brewery. Trade increased from month to month, licensed houses were acquired, and the business grew to one of considerable importance. Until its purchase by Taylor Walker & Co. at the end of 1929, the Brewery employed about 30 hands, possessed 15 licensed houses, and sold 16,000 barrels a year. (Information extracted from unpublished reminiscences of Alex Glenny). The 1st edition Ordnance Survey map shows the Stonehill Cottage Beer House, predecessor to the Thatched House, extending westwards, which probably indicates the route of the old road before the turnpike cut the corner in 1812.

Acres of Meadow land & let at a yearly rent of £55. In 1884 the tenant was a Mr Saunders & in 1885 (Sept) it was destroyed by fire & the same year the present bricked & tiled house erected. In May 1895, George Sawkins, a native of Rippleside, was challenged to walk from Southend to the Harrow in 6 hours. He completed the walk – 34 miles – in 5 hours 56[.5] minutes. George Sawkins was a farm worker, but became notorious locally as a rough walker. On an artificial track he was unsuccessful. Previously – in 1890 – he walked from the Golden Lion, Romford, to the Brittania, Barking – 7 miles – within the hour.

The Castle[75] – this castelated house – a poor imitation, stands at the corner of Upney Lane & [is] said to be built about 1800. It was for many years the residence of the Tyser family[76], but recent years – namely in 1907 – bills was displayed advertising that "Teas" & mineral waters was sold here. Nearly opposite is an house called White-Hall – a farm house having a long frontage & low pitched. It is entirely white-washed – hence its name. The owner is Mr Thomas Mills, Farmer[77].

---

75 Ripple Castle was built by Thomas Tyser between 1811 and 1814, and he was very pleased with it. Thomas Champness (1814-1888) was his grandson, for whose upbringing he was largely responsible. According to Linda O'Carroll, Mary Elizabeth Spashett married a son of Thomas Tyser, also called Thomas, who outlived her by many years, and probably married again. "It puzzles me, though, that he could have a father rich enough to build a house and call it a Castle, yet need to take up the risky life of a fisherman and spend many years of his life in Chancery, arguing over his late wife's inheritance – which he did" (Personal correspondence). Bert Lockwood says that Linda may be mistaken in thinking that Thomas Tyser was a rich man because he built the Castle. It was the strong wish of both his sons, Thomas and Edward, to go to sea, and the father Thomas helped the son Thomas to buy his own smack. Thomas Tyser junior married Mary Elizabeth Spashett in 1823; she died in childbirth on 30th June 1828, leaving two children. His father claimed the marriage was completely without his consent (although a few years earlier he had talked of "my friend Spashett", presumably referring to Elizabeth's father). Thomas senior became increasingly obsessed with the filial ingratitude of his eldest son, and in his manuscript memoirs (in the possession of Bert Lockwood) he recalls "the birth of a son, named Thomas, who in later days was born to be the curse of his family and him a very Judas Iscariot". The memoirs at this point are accompanied by a prose poem of ten and a half foolscap pages entitled "Depravity", relating the sins of Thomas against his father. Not until his son's second marriage to a Miss Preston in 1830 was the rest of the family able to bring about a reconciliation.

76 Thomas Tyser, Ripple Castle. (White's 1848, Kelly's 1851). Thomas Champness; Miss Tyser, Ripple Castle, Rippleside. (Kelly's 1871). Thomas Champness is listed in Axe Street in 1878 (Kelly's).

77 Thomas Mills, farmer, Ripple Hall; John Stock, cowkeeper, The Castle. (Kelly's 1890).

Rippleside. This spot commences this village & it extends about 2 miles from Barking Town boundary. Capt Perry[78] in his account of the Dagenham Gulph, calls it (in 1714) Ripley-side & his map only shows 5 or 6 buildings.

Moggs Farm. A short distance from the "White-Hall" is a modern double-fronted house with tiled roof occupied by Mr William Poole, with marshes attached to it. These marshes extending towards the Thames is called Ripple level. The immediate lands in the rear of the house – 10 acres – was granted in 1558 to a Thomas Argall & in 1585 Ferdinhand Richardson possessed it (Morant[79]). No doubt an old Farm-house stood on the site of the present one. The farm is no doubt named after Thomas & Agnes Mogge, [Page 415]

who with others demised in 1483 to Robert Wolfe, Skinner & Citizen of London two acres of land called "Crabbeland" in the marshes East of Barking, on conditions that certain monies was paid to a Church in London. In this demise was also mentioned some land in "Bakerstrate" Barking[80]: Wolfe, after the death of his wife Joan, granted them to Thomas Bedyngham of Barking, Gent (State papers).

The Ship & Shovel. This is a modern building of red-brick & is a well known house. In the past all kinds of sports was held here, especially pigeon shooting matches. Side of this house is a lane leading to the marshes & horse shoe Corner, so named from the shape of the grazing land there & a safe place for grazing of cattle[81]. The keys of the marshes was kept by a landlord

78   John Perry (1670-1732): *Account of the stopping of Daggenham Breach.* 1721.

79   Philip Morant *The history and antiquities of the County of Essex, compiled from the best and most ancient historians.* 2 vols. T. Osborne, 1768 & 2nd edition, 1816.

80   Baker(y)strete, so called in 1456, later known as Axe Street. Referred to as "le Axestreete alias Bakerstreete" in 1609. *Place-names of Essex.* 1935. p.89.

81   According to J. G. O'Leary, "horseshoes" cut in the bank of the river wall were part of the defensive measures to prevent the Thames flooding the marshes. *Dagenham place names.* 1958. p. 55. Here O'Leary failed to understand his sources, or at least to make his meaning clear. The "horseshoe" is, in fact, the semicircular dyke or embankment thrown up on the landward side to restrict the flooding of grazing land following a breach in the river wall. So Frogley is probably more correct about the meaning. The Horseshoe Corner referred to here lay in Dagenham just beyond the Barking boundary and is plainly marked on the Ordnance Survey 1st edition (6 and 25 inch) and later maps. It could be approached from Barking direction along Choats Manor Way, to which the Marsh Lane (alias Mogges Lane) beside the Ship and Shovel gave access.

Staff at the Glenny Brewery, Barking. (See footnote 74 on page 38).

Drawing of "Byfrons Mansion" in 1800. Page 223 in the manuscript.

The Congregational church - Page 287 in the manuscript. (See pages 134 - 137)

Frogley's drawing of the Chequers pub, on page 417 in the manuscript. (See page 51).

Frogley's delightful drawing of Church Path, on pages 62 - 63 in the manuscript.

Daniel Day's headstone, photographed in 1905. (See page 77).

Dagenham Dock in 1911. (See pages 160 - 161).

47

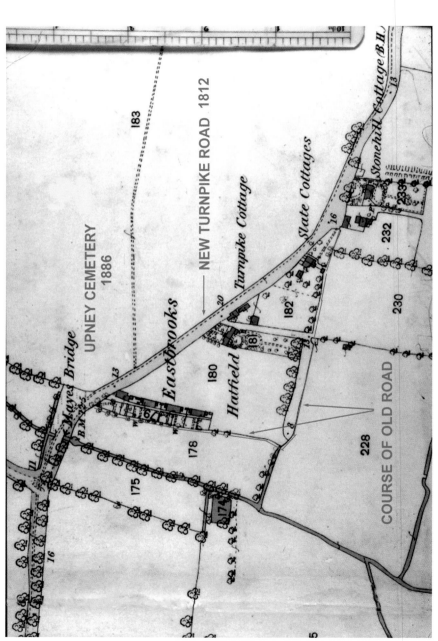

Stonehill Cottage beerhouse, the precursor of the Thatched House, shown on the 25 - inch OS map. (See pages 38 - 39).

48

of this house & singularly his name was Samuel "Keys"[82]. The licence here is very old – probably dating from 1740[83]. It was then a small house & later destroyed by fire & another erected on its site. The marshes at the rear, being so isolated, has in the past been used for many unlawful purposes. In the "Thirties"[84], says Mr Mathews, an old inhabitant of East-Ham, - (he refers to the 19th century) – some Barking men was mixed up in a smuggling case in which a cargo of Tobacco was landed not far from this house & was being carried accross the marshes, but the Revenue Authorities, having previously got news of it, they seized the carts & the men was sent to prison for 12 months. Also here on 13th March 1820 two pugilists named "Parrish" and "Hadbrook" fought a battle of 41 rounds & Parrish was the Conqueror. In 1883 a Mr G. Rowe sold it to a Mr Lane[85], who had just come away from the "Coach & Horses " Plaistow. The present landlord is Mr Charles King.

The Ship & Shovel[86] – Mr Glenny thinks[87] – was named after Sir Cloudesley Shovel. He was born in 1650 & rose from a Cabin boy rapidly until he became Admiral of the White Fleet. William III knighted him - & after a life of active service – in returning from a successful expedition against Toulon, his ship struck upon the rocks of Sicily[88] [on] Oct 22, 1707 & the Admiral with several others perished. His body was flung on the shore & with others buried in the sand, but soon after was taken up by command of his Royal

---

The origin is explained in the Survey of Dagenham Levels, 1563 (Essex Record Office D/SH 7). As a result of a breach in the Thames wall in 1556, 52.5 acres were flooded creating an inset of tidal salt-marsh called the Great Horseshoe because "The same Breach is defended by a wall called a Horse Shoe" (actually more rectangular than horseshoe shaped in this case).

82 His name is spelt variously: Samuel Key, Ship and Shovel. (White's 1848); Samuel Keeys. (Kelly's 1851); Samuel Keys. (Kelly's 1871). Trade also given as blacksmith in White 1848.

83 In fact, probably much earlier. William Foster and Mary Gillum, from "near the sign of the Shovel, Ripple Side, Barking", were married in September 1699. *Barking pubs past and present*. 1995. p.15.

84 1830s.

85 Frederick Curzon Lane, Ship & Shovel P.H. (Kelly's 1890).

86 It is possible that Sir Cloudesley Shovel could have had a pub named after him by 1699. He had been knighted after the Battle of Bantry Bay in 1689, was created a Rear Admiral in 1690, and was already a popular figure.

87 This is evidence that Frogley obtained information - written and/or verbal – probably from William Wallis Glenny.

88 Should be the Scilly Isles. *Barking record*, no.82.

Mistress & buried in St Peters Abbey Church, Westminster, where she caused a monument to be erected to his memory.

Opposite the Ship & Shovel is a few cottages. It was in one of these that the Sawkins family resided. One day- while all was away from home – in December 1906 their home was destroyed by fire. The damage was estimated at £100.

Scrattons Farm[89] comprises a modern erected farm-house & about 80 Acres of good land: viz 30 Arable & 50 Marsh. It abutts on the main road & was offered for sale in Sept 1896. Early in the 19th Century the "Scratton family" possessed "Porters" near Parsloes[90].

The Royal Oak. This house stands a few yards from the Chequers, & although a modern structure, the Licence I am informed is older than the Chequers. And if the name [Page 416] signifies anything it must be very old, commemorating the incident of King Charles hiding up an Oak tree. Formerly a cottage stood here & had the Licence but in 1880 it was demolished & the present neat building erected. The sign of the "Royal Oak" only occurs about 20 times in Essex.

Lodge Farm[91]. This farm-house stands a great distance from Ripple Road & is a substantially built brick building. In 1850 it was tenanted by Mr Henry Gray[92] & his family in 1906 possessed a farm near the Chequers. After

---

89   The former name of Scrattons Farm was Oskyns Hawe, dating back at least to the 13th century. The Old English name "Hawe" signifies a "houseground". "Three acres called Oskyns Hawe lying near Rippleside" are mentioned in 1609. Edmund Surrey was farming Scrattons in 1890 (Kelly's). The conveyance of Scrattons Farm to the London County Council dated 9th May 1922 was accompanied by a statutory declaration that "The Scrattons" was formerly known by the name of *Oskinshaugh*. Another accompanying deed shows that it had been conveyed under the old name as late as 1875. An old thatched cowshed and barn were said to be ruinous on this site in 1901. (Partly extracted from personal correspondence from Herbert Lockwood).

90   James Scratton, Surveyor, Ripple Ward, 1805-6; Overseer, 1807; Churchwarden, 1812. *Barking vestry minutes*. 1955. p.324.

91   According to Herbert Lockwood, Lodge Farm, also known as Porters Lodge Farm, was on or near the site of the ancient manor house of Porters. In the course of the 17th century the lands of this manor came under the same ownership as the adjoining estates of Jenkins and Longbridge. The name Porters was dropped in favour of Porters Lodge during the later 17th century, which suggests that the old house had already been pulled down. Great Porters, in Gale Street, though nearby, had no connection with the manor of Porters, but took its name from a family who acquired it in the 16th century.

92   Henry Gray, farmer, Lodge Farm. (Kelly's 1851).

leaving Lodge Farm, he became connected with the Morgan Dairy Company[93] and I was informed that they erected the viaduct by which the "sewerage matter" was conveyed overland from the Northern Outfall to this farm[94]. By this method the ground was periodically soaked & it was possible to force – in some cases – t[w]o crops a year. Grass for instance. Mr Walter Mills now possesses this farm[95].

Starland Hall. A delapidated farm house, near the Chequers & stands alone in a field some distance from the main road. By its appearance most probably it was a century ago the residence of some respectable Farmer, but when the writer visited it in 1900 a tenant – or caretaker - said it was difficult to get anyone to reside there.

The Chequers[96] - a sign of great antiquity & is common in Essex. There is many suggestions as to the origination of this sign – some even suggesting the ruins of "Pompeii" with its checked floors &c – but no doubt the Ale-house sign in England, originates from the "Checky" arms of the Earls of Warren & Surrey, who possessed for several reigns the privilege of Licensing houses of Entertainment in England.

Originally the above house was painted in large black & white checks, but [in] recent years they have been painted out. The Chequers is well known, especially to Anglers that fished in the "Gulf" close by. The lane leading from this house to the Gulf was called "Sickle Lane". In 1898 I was informed by an old resident near there, that originally the Chequers stood some

---

93 The Metropolitan Sewage & Essex Reclamation Company (incorporated by Act of Parliament) took control of Lodge Farm during the later 1860s. Henry J. Morgan was their Secretary and H. W. Petre was manager. Raw sewage was siphoned under the Roding from the Northern Outfall works and, with the assistance of a steam pump, fed into a raised cistern on the farm, from which it was distributed to the fields by gravity along wooden and iron troughs on trestles. Average applications were 4,000 tons per acre per annum, and the production of animal feed and crops was impressive (there is a detailed report in *Essex Times*, 3rd October 1868). In 1873 the experiment was blamed for an outbreak of typhoid in the locality. See: J. E. Oxley, "Barking town and London sewage" in *Essex Journal*, vol.22, 1987, p.57-61.

94 For a description of this method of fertilisation using sewage, see the notes by Tony Clifford accompanying *Essex (new series): sheet 86.04: Upney 1915* in the Alan Godfrey series of old Ordnance Surveys maps (ISBN 0850549493).

95 Frederick Stevens, foreman to Mr Walter Mills, Rippleside. (Kelly's 1890).

96 For a history of the Chequers pub, see Tony Clifford: *Dagenham pubs past and present*. 1996. p.6-8.

distance up the opposite lane – nearer to Dagenham[97], & the Licence was transferred to the present spot. My informant said he had in recent years seen the ruins of the old house. If this is correct, most probably the licence was transferred to this spot in about 1810 – when the new road – Dagenham New Road – was made, thus connecting Ripple Road with Rainham[98]. Dagenham New Road commences from the Chequers & proceeds to Rainham. The Gulf is noticed seperately. Having gone to the extent of Ripple Road I will now return to Upney Lane.

Upney-Lane (sometimes called Lodge Lane). This picturesque lane connects Ripple Road with Longbridge Road. There is not much to notice in it except the Isolation Hospital. [Page 418] Years ago it was a favorite walk from the Town accross Faircross Farm by a narrow footpath to Upney Lane. Here still stands some old cottages & in the garden of one of them was a famous Mulberry Tree, that yielded abundance of fruit. There is also a foot-path from here to Lodge Farm.

The Isolation Hospital. During the 19th Century these splendid Institutions has greatly increased, & every Local Authority now either establishes one, or joins another Authority for that purpose. But Barking in 1678-80 possessed a Charity-House or Local Hospital, kept by one John Clements. It received cases from the surrounding districts that Doctors considered required other treatment (History of Dagenham[99]). The above Hospital is situated on the site of a beautiful meadow & adjoining was two cottages (still standing). In August 1892 the Barking & East-Ham Councils had a conference in reference to a joint Hospital accommodation for Infectious diseases for the two Districts, & their respective Clerks was directed to get certain facts or statistics from similar authorities – find a suitable site &c. Their report suggested 6 Acres of land in the Barking Road at £200 an Acre.

---

97 Most probably the junction today of Broad Street and Ford Road, Dagenham. *Dagenham pubs past and present.* p.7.

98 New Road, a turnpike road leading to Tilbury Fort, was built as a defensive measure during the Napoleonic Wars.

99 John Peter Shawcross: *A history of Dagenham in the County of Essex.* 1904. p.26, where the name is given as James Clement. But Shawcross himself probably misunderstood an entry in the 1679/80 Manorial survey (now Essex Record Office D/DHs M81 fo.21), which says that Jacob Clement of London, Scrivener, was Master of "the Charity House called the Hospital of Great Ilford". Frogley has increased the confusion here. There is no evidence that the ancient Hospital of Ilford ever provided any medical treatment.

1 Bed for each 2000 inhabitants (estimated then at 50,000) & permanent provision for 8 Small-Pox beds.

The cost of laying out lands & Buildings was estimated at £6200.

The Councils on considering the above Report regarded the site as the most important feature – and at another conference of the two Councils nothing was definatly settled. Later Barking Council acted by themselves, & proposed to erect at Upney a temporary structure or large Tents at a cost of £73. This was in 1893, but March, same year, it was decided to erect for temporary purposes Iron buildings at a cost of £127 – or a total when finished of £181. This was done & in November 1893 it was further decided to purchase the above Upney Meadow for £1350, also that Dr Gibbens[100] be appointed Medical Officer at a Salary of £20 a year & that he be paid £10 for services rendered at the Temporary Hospital. The new building was at once proceeded with & finished at a cost of £1000. There are two sets of Buildings – one for Fever & one for Small-Pox, the former accommodating 12 & the latter 8 patients. The buildings are of Corrugated Iron & [were] erected by Messrs Humphreys & Co. In Jan 1894 a Caretaker was appointed at a Salary of £78 per ann[um], with house, coals & uniform.

Rippleside[101]. [Pages 301-302]

This village in the 15th century was called "Rippell" and Capt Perry[102] in his report on Dagenham Gulf calls it "Ripley-side" & at which time (1714) [it] contained about 12 houses. It is situated about [1.5] miles from Barking but it extends some 2 miles along the Ripple Road. There were several Manor Houses or Farms in this district, but they, with the Recreation Ground, Cemetery &c is spoken of seperately. After the passing of the Union Act in 1834 it became a part & parcel of the old Parish of Barking. In 1881-2, on the formation of the Barking Local Board, Rippleside became a Local Government District & in 1885 (Sept 29) a Provisional Order was obtained

100 Frank Edward Gibbens, physician & surgeon, 10 Cambridge Road. (Kelly's 1890).

101 P. H. Reaney, in *The place-names of Essex*, p.89, derives Rippleside from the Old English *rippel*, a "strip", in this case the higher land along Ripple Road, north of the marshes and Ripple Level. Ripple was one of the four wards of the ancient parish of Barking.

102 John Perry (1670-1732).

whereby Rippleside was added to the Local Board District of Barking with one Member to represent it on that body. The first member was Mr E. H. Waltham, Farmer[103].

In 1811, it contained 57 houses & population about 267

In 1831   73   387

197 Males & 190 females

In 1851   435

In 1871[104]

In 1891

In 1911

Rippleside School. Previous to 1860 there appears to have been no school at this village – the children then walked to Barking - but the late Francis Whitbourn Esqr built a School there & surported [it][105]. He also promised to support it so long as it continued [as] a voluntary school. At a meeting of the School Board in Dec 1895, Mr Mason[106], a member, proposed that suitable accommodation be provided at Rippleside, but nothing was then decided until Jan[uar]y 1896, when inhabitants there petitioned the Board for a School. The old School building [was] then rented by the Vicar of Barking who agreed to let it to the Board. Having decided to build a new School at Rippleside the Board in April 1896 advertised for tenders & the following was received. Architect C. J. Dawson.

103 Edward Waltham, farmer, Maybells. (Kelly's 1878); Edward Hawkins Waltham, farmer, Maybells Farm. (Kelly's 1890).

104 Frogley does not provide the statistics beyond 1851. The population in 1861 was about 350 (Kelly's 1871), in 1871 about 515 (Kelly's 1878) and in 1881 about 1,138 (Kelly's 1890).

105 Francis Whitbourne, miller, Wellington Mill. (Kelly's 1878).

106 Hugh Herbert Mason, surgeon & certifying factory surgeon & medical officer & public vaccinator, No.3 district, Romford Union, Abbey Lodge, East Street. (Kelly's 1890). Dr Mason represented Barking on the Essex County Council from 1892.

	For School	For Class Rooms
Messrs M. N. Hawkins	£2983	£456
Messrs J. J. Horlock	£3071	£405
Messrs J. Smith[107]	£3297	£510
Messrs T. Bruley [?]	£3109	£418
Messrs H. J. Carter	£2938	£448
Messrs J. Hammond & Son	£2875	£449 = Accepted
Messrs Turtle & Appleton	£2875	£450
Messrs Kirk & Randall	£3153	£497
Messrs Stillwell & Manning	£3050	£460

The site upon which this School stands measures three-quarters of an Acre in extent. It has a frontage to the main Ripple Road of 200 feet & a return frontage to Lodge Lane of over 100 feet, Lodge Lane having been widened to 40 feet for the length of the School premises. The building is designed as a mixed school for boys & girls & infants – being planned on the Central-Hall & class room principles, providing accommodation for 120 boys, 120 girls and 76 Infants – a total of 316 children. The Central Hall is 61 feet long & 24 feet 6 [inches] wide. At one end there is accommodation for 60 Children. The other classes are accommodated in the two classrooms on each side. Seperate & distinct entrances & cloakrooms are provided for each department of the school – that for the girls being on the South front & for the boys & girls on the East & West sides respectively. The Cloakrooms are fitted with numbered Caps & Cloak hooks, Lavatory Basin &c. A private room for the use of the Teachers is provided to the right of the South entrance. The Classrooms, teachers private room & central Hall are warmed by open fire lump grates known as the "Marlboroughs". The system of ventilation is by simple inlet & outlet, the whole of the window being of a special design whereby the lower sash being slightly raised an upward current of air is admitted at the Sill & meeting bar levels, the whole width of the window within causing unpleasant draughts, whilst for summer ventilation both the lower sashes can be opened to their full extent. Also the sashes above these, which are hung on centres & fitted with iron gearing for

107 John Smith, builder, Wishford House, Longbridge Road. (Kelly's 1890).

opening & closing same, as are also the fanlights over the doorways. A seperate flue for carrying of the inhaled vitiated air from the upper part of the classrooms & central Hall is carried with the smoke flues. These are fitted near the ceiling with louvre ventilators. The internal space of walls to classrooms & central Hall has a cement dado with a capping of reeded glazed bricks & the upper portion is faced with stocks & distempered. The floors of the Classrooms & Central Hall – excepting under the seats – are formed with wood blocks laid herring-bone fashion on concrete. The floors of entrance Porch, Cloakrooms & lavatories are paved with tiles also laid herring bone fashion. The exterior of the building is faced to a height of 4 feet 6 inches from ground line with pressed red bricks & above them with yellow stocks largely relieved with red bricks. The roof is covered with Strawberry red Broseley plain tiles & surmounted with a bell turret & vane. The Playground is partly enclosed with a substantial brick wall & partly with iron pallisading & the ground paved with limestone tar paving.

The School was formerly opened by Mr H. Berry[108] – Vice Chairman of the School Board – on 28th May 1897.

As agriculture is still carried on around this district, a few remarks upon that industry may be interesting especially as it is an industry that so flourished at Barking, but for some years past the once thriving farms are now converted into building estates, recreation grounds &c. The marshes for grazing was also very valuable and is so at the present time, but many of these are near the sites of factories & houses in consequence. In 1800 it was computed that there were 1980 Acres of Marsh land & 250 acres of Grass lands which produced hay. These latter was let at rents averaging from £7 to £10 per Acre. Also in the Parish – from a Report made in 1783 upon "Woods"[109] - it was computed that there were 11055 oak trees of 10 feet & upwards & 2760 trees of 30 feet & upwards & thousands smaller. They were reccommended & finally cut down for the Navy – the same being carted to the Town Quay at 5/- a load.

---

108 Henry Berry, Linden Villa, Linton Road. (Kelly's 1890). On page 274 of the manuscript, Frogley writes: "Henry Berry, Clerk at Beckton Works. Member of Local Board from 1898 & District Council. He is said to represent the Beckton Gas Company".

109 Barking & Dagenham Libraries have *The first report of the Commissioners appointed to enquire into the state and condition of the woods, forests and land revenues of the Crown and to sell or alienate fee farm and other unimproveable rents*, dated 25th January 1787.

Also about 1800 there was estimated to be upwards of 5000 Acres of Arable land under cultivation by Farmers. This land produced Wheat, Tares[110], Clover, Carrots, Cabbages, Potatoes &c. The soil of this Parish varied, but there were two kinds more marked (Page[111]).   [Page 303]

Some parts of it is dry & Turnips was grown plentifully. Another kind consisted of heavy clay & required continual draining. Mr Lysons[112] says that there were 150 acres of cabbages here & 600 acres of Potatoes. At this time (about 1800 & later) Agriculture was at its highest point. Also for many years later, there were in the Parish several large farmers, employing the bulk of the inhabitants. Some I would mention in the District around Barking [are] Mr Thomas Mathews[113], Mr Cobb, Mr T. Circuit (who it is said introduced methods of Farming prevailent in Lancashire). They were at East-Ham. Also the families of Whitbourn[114] – Mead[115] – Hunsdon – Gray[116] – Peacock[117] – Glenny[118] – Pittman[119] – Newman & many others mentioned under the various farms they possessed. An interesting account is given upon Potatoes by Page, viz:-

110 Vetches.

111 William Page (1861-1934), antiquarian, historian and editor of the Victoria County History of Essex.

112 Daniel Lysons *The environs of London*. T. Cadell, 1796. Supplementary volume (1811), p.339.

113 Frogley provides a footnote on page 2 of the manuscript relating to Thomas Mathews: "Mr Thomas Mathews of East-Ham, Farmer. He was alive in 1904, and retired to Romford, after residing at East Ham, his native place.The ancient History of East-Ham was his great study"

114 William F. Whitbourn, Loxford Hall. (White 1848).

115 Frederick Mead, farmer, Great Porters, Rippleside. (Kelly's 1871).

116 Henry Gray, farmer. (White 1848).

117 John P. Peacock, farmer, Longbridge. (Kelly's 1851).

118 For example, Charles, John, William, Thomas and Edward Glenny, farmers and market gardeners. (White 1848).

119 Thomas Pittman (d.1760) was farming Loxford by 1732, but a William Pittman was there in the mid-18th century. (It seems to have been the custom in the family to name the eldest son Thomas and the second William). He was succeeded by another Thomas Pittman who died in 1791, and it was his son Thomas whose progressive farming methods won the admiration of Arthur Young in his survey of the agriculture of Essex, written in 1807. *VCH Essex: vol.5*. p.206. This latter Thomas died in 1818 when he was thrown from his chaise at Bow Bridge on the night of 17th February, and apparently his own son Thomas died later that year. In the early 19th century other Pittmans were farming Upney and Jenkins.

Potatoes were cultivated more in Essex than in any other Southern county & Ilford was the centre. A particular potato – the Champions – had the preference. Mr Thomas Pittman of Loxford Hall about 1807 alone had 300 acres under crop & he was considered the most enterprising & largest grower. His yield was 7 tons per acre & 10 tons from land he had on the Dagenham marshes, where he possessed 40 acres of land & the soil was called "Black Marl"[120]. He invented a plough or rather he really improved upon one which displaced hoeing by hand. It is singular that the Essex men have always & is now the best ploughers in the Country. What was considered extraordinary he washed his potatoes & for this purpose he sank a well at a cost of £200. He also built at Loxford a Bullocks house capable of holding 100 Oxens & which he fed with his surplus potatoes. He was also a large breeder of Swine, having at one time 600 head of a Berkshire sort & he possessed a Boar & Sow which he challenged against all England for £100.

Speaking of Oxen, the same authority (Mr Young[121]) says that a Mr Walters of Alborough Hatch, Farmer, had no horses on his farm, but employed Oxen only to do his work. They even went to London & back the same day & gave him general satisfaction. They were of a Devon Breed. There appears to be no special "Essex" breed of live stock but in the various markets all kinds are represented. In 1807- adjoining Hainhault Forest – the East India Company possessed some 108 acres of land for the purpose of breeding horses of which they had then about 100 horses. The Company stocked their possessions in this manner in their Eastern Countries.

Agriculture no doubt gradually improved from importations of various kinds of roots into this country. At one time as land was cleared & brought into cultivation the fields were entirely open. Rapin[122] says that the Saxons divided the land by ditches, some of which were banked & which formed a boundary, but still the fields remained comparatively open until the 15th Century when land that was rendered fit for ploughing were divided by hedges & this was carried on for 3 centuries later. A more marked system of Market gardening was in 1590 introduced by the Flemish & Dutch.

---

120 Marl is soil consisting of clay and carbonate of lime, a valuable fertiliser.

121 Arthur Young: *General view of the agriculture of the County of Essex*. 2 vols. 1807.

122 Paul de Rapin-Thoyras: *The history of England*. Various editions are listed in the British Library catalogue of printed books. According to John Kenyon, Rapin's History "established itself as the nearest thing to a standard history of England". *The history men* 1983. The 1789 edition is available in the Guildhall Library.

The first Flemish gardens proved highly successful. Their cabbages, carrots & celery had a ready sale. They first settled at Sandwich, Kent, but such were the demands in the London Markets that they also settled at Wandsworth, Bermondsey & Battersea. Asparagus was first grown at Battersea by the Flemish. A very common vegetable singularly not known in this country previous to 1800 was "Rhubarb". A Mr Myatt of Deptford in 1820 cultivated it there & he carried 7 bundles to the Borough Market, but only sold 3 bundles, as everyone thought they were Physic[123].

The Churchyard. [Pages 119-133]

In this Country it is said that the Romans had their burial places in the fields & highways, as by a law of the XII Tables[124] burying between walls was expressively forbidden. In A.D.210 – under Pope Calixtus[125] – places of burial was consecrated. Also among the primitive Christians, cemeteries was held in great veneration, but burying in Churches was prohibited for centuries by Christian Emperors. The first step towards this was the erection of buildings over the graves of Martyrs in the cemeteries – or the translation of Relics of others in the Churches or Cities. Later Emperors & Kings was buried in the porches. It is said that the first Christian Burial was instituted in 596: & in churches in 742: in consecrated places 750 & in Churchyards in 758, some however states that Churchyards was so used in the 6th century. Vaults was first erected in Churches – at Canterbury – in 1075 & the earliest monuments was probably flat stones. In 1666 woolen shrouds [were] first used. In 1695 Burials was taxed, viz:- a Duke £30 & a common person 4/-[126].

The date & origin of Barking Churchyard, but it is very ancient. According to the Venerable Bede, it originated through a vision, at a time when the

---

123 Medicine.

124 The earliest code of Roman law, engraved on twelve bronze tablets.

125 The catacombs of St. Callixtus are among the greatest and most important of Rome. They originated about the middle of the second century and are part of a complex which occupies an area of 90 acres, with a network of galleries about 12 miles long, in four levels, more than twenty metres deep. In it were buried tens of martyrs, 16 popes and very many Christians. They are named after the Deacon Callixtus who, at the beginning of the third century, was appointed by Pope Zephyrinus as the administrator of the cemetery, and so the catacombs of St. Callixtus became the official cemetery of the Church of Rome.

126 Four shillings, now 20 pence.

inmates of the Abbey was suffering terribly of a plague that raged all over East Anglia, therefore this spot was used as a burial place for about 1200 years. It was in 1884 that Dr Hoffman of the Home Office inspected the Churchyard, & after his report, the Home Office ordered it to be closed against burials from 31st March 1885 – excepting where there was room in the family graves then existing. Originally, after passing through the Curfew Tower, the Churchyard was open, but in 1883 the present iron fence was erected at a cost of £35. The Mortuary – now a tool house – stands at the North West corner of the Churchyard & the North-wall from this spot contains many Roman tiles, said to come from the old Abbey.

Body-snatching. [Page 119]

The late Mr Thomas Mathews of East-Ham said that some 60 years ago there was a gang of bodysnatchers in Barking – seven or eight of them - & [they] got their living by it. They worked Barking, East Ham & Little Ilford & in those days, when anyone was buried, it was usual to watch the grave for some days. In 1827-8 a Mrs Kingshott died & a farm labourer was accosted by three men, who questioned him so that he guessed their intentions & went to Mr Kingshott & warned him to watch the grave. Accordingly he put eight men to watch & about 9 oclock at night three men appeared, went to the grave & commenced to dig. Out rushed the watchers & caught the three, bound them with ropes & dragged them backwards and forwards through a pond close-by in East-Ham. This pond was near the old Church. They were afterwards taken to Barking Jaol & later sentenced to a term of imprisonment. The Magistrate was Mr Sp[urrell]. The writer has been told of several instances of Body-snatching taken place at Barking, by old inhabitants[127].

[Memorials in the Churchyard][128].

1682 Thomas. Bailiff to Henry Wight[129] Esqre of Gayshams. He was a native of Sussex.

---

127 In 1823, John Hughes of Barking registered a patent entitled *Securing bodies in coffins*, a deterrent against body snatchers. (Patent specification no.4843 AD 1823, published by Eyre & Spottiswoode, for the Patent Office, 1856). See also: Alfred Stokes: *History of East Ham* (1933), p.136-137.

128 On pages 118-133, Frogley gives a list of gravestones in Barking churchyard, with biographical notes. He does not explain how he came to write this section and it is

1689 Young, Jane. Daughter of Edward & Mary Young, died 16 Feb 1689[130]. This family resided at Cranbrooke[131]. A son, Lewis Young of Cranbrooke & Bampton, Oxfordshire married Elizabeth, daughter of James Medlicott, Esq of London.

1573. Knight, Sir Robert of Ilford[132].

1693. Casson, Ann. – daughter of William Casson (below), died 7th Nov[133].

1705. Casson, William, died 31st January.

1742. Hinde, Ruth, daughter of William Casson (above) & wife of Henry Hinde Esqre of West-Ham. This memorial is attached to the Small Wall of the Church.

1748. Pelly, John. Also his wife Sarah, 1748 & three infant children – being all the children of Captain John & Elizabeth Pelly[134].

1706. Bennett, Capt John, Senr. Age 70. This is an Alter Tomb, & I give here the inscription taken from the splendid Monument in the Church:

---

transcribed here in the order it appears in the manuscript. It seems unlikely that he had the time to survey the churchyard himself, and a full survey of extant headstones was not carried out until 1930. There is some evidence that somebody else transcribed the headstones, which may account for the numerous inaccuracies. Many inscriptions would have been more easily readable in Frogley's day than in 1930, but were almost certainly checked out more carefully in the later official survey. For this reason, double-checking against burial registers and other sources such as wills and manorial records is advised when trying to trace ancestors.

129 Henry Wight died in 1698, having inherited Gayshams from his father Gabriel (d.1621). The Wight family owned the manor of Gayshams, in whole or part, from 1609 to 1873.

130 According to the 1930 survey, she died on 20th January 1689, aged 16 years 3 months.

131 See: *VCH Essex: Vol.5.* 1966. p.198.

132 On page 92 of the manuscript, Frogley writes: " Sir Robert Knight was seated at Ilford, and a descendant, also Sir Robert Knight, was cashier to the South Sea Company & he purchased Luxborough Manor near Chigwell, and afterwards built the Manor House, but his Estates were seized & sold by the Company. He however repurchased them in 1740 & dying in 1744 was succeeded by his son, who in 1746 was created Baron Luxborough & in 1763 an Irish Peer. This Manor which adjoined Clayhall was purchased by James Hatch Esqr of Clayhall (see Clayhall)".

133 According to the 1930 survey, she was aged 3 years 8 months, and buried on the north side of the church.

134 According to the 1930 survey, John Pelly, aged 5 years 4 months, died on 20th October 1748. His sister, Sarah, aged 2 years 5 months, died on 20th September 1748. A very dubious transcription!

"To the pious memory of Capt John Bennett Senr who died 8th May 1706 Age 70 & Mary his wife who died 2nd January 1711 age 74 – both lying here interred. Also Capt John Bennett their eldest son who died 3rd January 1716[135] age 46 & lyeth in a Vault under an Alter Tomb in the Churchyard – and ordered by his Will that this monument be erected, who also left £100 to the poor of this Parish".

1711. Bennett, Mary, wife of above. Age 74.

1716. Bennett, Capt John. Son of above. Age 46[136].

1729. Vere, William. Bricklayer[137]. Also his son Thomas[138].

1719. Jelfe, John. Gent. (See Monuments in Church)[139].

1709. Kempton, William, of Great Ilford[140].

1720. Kempton, Samuel, of Great Ilford[141].

1747. Knight, Esther & her husband William (date nearly gone[142]). Citizen & Draper.

1749. Horderne, Thomas[143]. He married Susan daughter of Robert Smith, Miller of Barking (her 2nd husband).

---

135 30th January 1716 according to the 1930 survey.

136 A good example of Frogley repeating himself for no apparent reason.

137 According to the 1930 survey, he died 13th November 1729, aged 53.

138 Thomas Vere, Overseer, Barking, 1751; Churchwarden, 1750-1. *Barking vestry minutes.* 1955. p.326.

139 John Jelfe, Surveyor, Barking, 1701; Overseer, Barking and Ripple, 1714; Churchwarden, Barking, 1717-19. *Barking vestry minutes.* 1955. p.322. Later mentions of John Jelfe in Oxley's index are presumably a relative. According to the 1930 survey, John Jelfe died on 2nd April 1743, aged 49, "and near this place are 7 of his children". John Jelfe – sometimes spelt "Gelf" – was an 18th century tenant of Malmaynes of Ripple. The only Jelfe monument within St Margaret's Church, Barking, is a ledger stone to Nicholas Jelfe (d.1758) and his son Thomas (d.1789).

140 According to the 1930 survey, he died 1st November 1709, aged 73.

141 Samuel Kempton, Churchwarden, Ilford, 1711; Overseer, Ilford, 1713. *Barking vestry minutes.* 1955. p.322. According to the 1930 survey, he died 31st March 1720, aged 73 "and upwards".

142 The 1930 survey gives the date as 1767.

143 The 1930 survey gives his occupation as surgeon, died 15th March 1750, aged 32.

1786. Moungall, Susan, previous wife of Thomas Horderne who died 1750 (above). She was the da[ughter] of Robert Smith, Miller.

1747. Smith, Robert of Abbey Mills, Barking[144]. His father Robert Smith was also a Miller of Poplar & Rotherhithe.

1784. Smith, Charles[145]. Son of Robert Smith, Miller of Barking & also his wife Hannah[146] who died in Oct 1775.

Dangerfield, Henry

Dangerfield, William   Date obliterated, but I assume their death took place in the 18th century as William in 1740 was landlord of the Rising Sun, Ilford[147].

1772. Stradling, Richard[148].

1769. Jessop, Richard, Gent of Ilford. He left by Will £300 in Stock & £191 due upon Mortgage towards the purchase of an Organ for Barking Church[149]. He also left £10 to the poor of the Parish.

1773. Jones, Gilbert, Gent. (I believe the date should be 1713)[150].

(See Monuments in Church).

---

144 The 1930 survey gives date of death as 6th February 1747, aged 89.

145 The 1930 survey gives date of death as 7th September 1784, aged 55.

146 The 1930 register lists Hannah Smith, who died 28th October 1775, aged 78. But whose wife was she? Was there another generation on this memorial missed both by Frogley and the compilers of the 1930 register?

147 This headstone again proved indecipherable in 1930 except for the two names. There were, however, three headstones (HD 1839, WD 1839, GD 1844). Frogley shows that he was aware that one Henry Dangerfield died in 1839 (see: *Mr Frogley's Barking: a first selection* (2002), p.15).

148 Richard Stradling, Overseer, Barking, 1749; Churchwarden, 1751-2; Surveyor, 1753. *Barking vestry minutes.* 1955. p.325. According to the 1930 survey, he died on 23rd May 1774, aged 73.

149 *VCH Essex: Vol.5*, p.227, gives the name as Richard Jessup.

150 According to the 1930 survey, Gilbert Jones died on 26th November 1713, aged 64. This entry proves conclusively that Frogley used a list prepared by someone else, but checked some of it himself.

1665. Porter, Stephen[151].

1774. Porter, Thomas.

1772. Porter, Mary (wife of Thomas).

1782. Porter, William. Age 63.

1796. Porter, Thomas. Brother of William.

There are several more tomb-stones of this family in the Churchyard. This family appears to have originated in Barking from a Stephen Parker, of London, Grocer, who married Margaret, daughter of ------- Smith of London, Gent. Their son Stephen, Gent, of Barking, married Anne, daughter of Anthony & Judith Bradshaw. This Stephen died in 1665 leaving children viz Anthony: William: Thomas: John: Arthur & 3 others. Anthony Bradshaw resided in London & by his wife Judith had 3 sons & 2 daughters, of whom – Anne – married Stephen Porter & the other daughter married a Thomas Lake of Barking in 1642 & their children was baptized at Barking. Some of the Lake family also resided at Little Ilford. Anthony Bradshaw dying was buried at Stifford Essex & his widow left London to reside at Barking, as described in her Will. After her death, she also was buried at Stifford.

1750. Guise, Ralph[152].

1751. Guise, Richard[153].

1763. Stone, Richard, of this Parish & whose ancestors possessed Ilford Hospital[154].

1769. Cocking, John, M.D[155]. His daughter Ann married Poulton Allan of Barking. (Also his wife Mary).

---

151 The Porter family, which included Stephen Porter (d.1665), gave their name to Great and Little Porters in Gale Street, Dagenham. Frogley's information appears to derive from the will of Stephen Porter (Essex Record Office D/AER 21/124), but Bert Lockwood is not sure whether the 18th century Porters were descendants of this family.

152 According to the 1930 survey died 11th April 1750.

153 Richard Guise, Overseer, Ilford, 1738; Churchwarden, 1741. *Barking vestry minutes*. 1955. p.321. According to the 1930 survey, he was the elder brother of Ralph Guise, and died in December 1762, aged 61.

154 According to the 1930 survey, Richard Stone, of London, banker, died on 29th May 1763, aged 59. His wife, Mary, died 13th October 1782, aged 75.

155 According to the 1930 survey, John Cocking, surgeon, died on 23rd June 1769, aged 55.

The memorial to Elizabeth and Joseph Fry, formerly in the Friends burial ground, Barking. (See pages 143).

BARKING, ESSEX.

FREEHOLD FAMILY RESIDENCE, STABLING, COTTAGE, OUTBUILDINGS, &c., AND ELIGIBLE BUILDING LAND.

MR. W. H. COLLIER

Is instructed by the British Land Company (Limited), to Offer by Auction, at the Mart, Tokenhouse Yard, City, E.C., on Monday, November 15th. at 2 precisely, in Four Lots,

THE FREEHOLD FAMILY RESIDENCE, situate at Rippleside, Barking, about five minutes' walk from Barking Railway Station, known as Westbury, containing ten bedrooms, dressing room, study, entrance and inner halls, drawing room, dining room, breakfast room, kitchen, bath room, usual domestic offices, and good cellarage; near to the residence is a large brick building, comprising billiard room, washhouse, and coal, wood, and knife houses. Large garden in front and paddock in rear. Also a six-roomed Cottage and excellent stabling, and Two Lots of Freehold Building Land, with frontages to Rippleside Road. The purchase-money may be paid by a deposit of 10 per cent., and the balance can remain on mortgage or contract at 5 per cent. interest, to be paid in nine years by equal half-yearly instalments; but the whole or any part of the balance may be paid off at any time without notice. Free conveyances will be given on the vendor's title being accepted.

The residence may be viewed, and particulars, plans, and conditions of Sale obtained on the Premises; of Messrs. R. and A. Russell, Solicitors, 59, Coleman Street, London, E.C.; of the Auctioneer, at the Offices of the British Land Company (Limited), 25, Moorgate Street, E.C.; and at the Place of Sale.

Advertisement in the Essex Times, 1880, regarding the sale of Westbury House. (See page 35).

The Royal Oak at Faircross. (See page 15).

Frogley's drawing of Faircross Farm on page 463 of the manuscript. (See pages 25 - 26).

The reverse of Daniel Day's headstone, photographed in 1905. (See page 77).

THOMAS FORGE,

WATCH AND CLOCK MAKER,

SILVERSMITH AND JEWELLER,

HIGH STREET, BARKING, & EAST HAM.

Watches, Clocks, Musical Boxes, Nautical Instruments, &c., accurately and promptly repaired and regulated.

Newspapers and Periodicals Regularly Supplied

DEALER IN TOBACCO.

AGENT FOR THE "ESSEX TIMES."

See pages 84 - 85

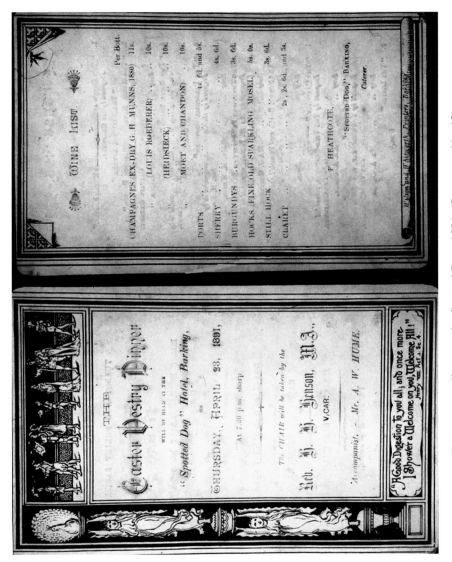

Easter vestry dinner at the Spotted Dog, 1891. (See pages 11 - 12)

Photograph showing the rebuilding of the Harrow pub in 1921, with the old building awaiting demolition. (See page 38).

1742. Gayer, Elizabeth, wife of Robert Gayer. (Son of Robert Gayer Knt).

1792. Tebb, Richard[156].

1793. Bray, Anna, wife of Samuel Bray Esqr.

1746. Bratten, James, Esqr.

1792. Keeling, Joseph[157]. Collector of Customs & his wife Sarah who died
1828 Age 96. For a description of this family see "Westbury" which he possessed together with the Abbey site: Perrymans: Cricklewood &c.

1790. Newman, Rebecca

1792. Newman, Thomas of Eastbury House, & I believe was the last representative of this family who occupied East-bury for 3 generations. (See Eastbury House)[158].

1739. Coulbourn, Nicholas. Gent of Barking. This family originated from Lancashire, and previous to coming to Barking, resided at Watford, Herts. Nicholas Coulbourn, father of [the] above, died in 1737 & his widow again married to Mr John Waldond of Barking, both of whom died in 1747. (See below Waldron family). (An Error – Mrs Waldron was wife (not mother) of Nicholas Coulbourn who died 1739)[159].

1747. Waldron, Elizabeth, relict of Nicholas Colbourn who died 1739 – her second husband. Her first husband – John Waldron of Barking – died

---

Mary, his wife, died on 1st October 1744, aged 23. Mrs Ann Allen, "relict of Poulton Allen Esq", died on 24th January, aged 84.

156 According to the 1930 survey, Richard Tebb died in February 1792, aged 42. Another Richard Tebb (d.1869) is also listed.

157 Joseph Keeling bought the manor of Westbury from Bamber Gascoyne in 1747. *VCH Essex: vol.5*. p.213. The 1930 survey lists Joseph Keeling, Collector of Customs of Barbados, who died on 23rd April 1792, aged 58. Alice Keeling, his widow, died on 23rd April 1823, aged 96.

158 See *Barking vestry minutes*. 1955. p.323 for several Thomas Newmans. It is not easy to unravel these frequent instances of repetitive names.

159 The family name should be spelt Walrond. The Coulburn/Walrond monument was worn but partly decipherable in 1930. Frogley's two paragraphs about this are so confused that it may be useful to quote the register: "Here lyeth interr'd the Body of Nicholas, only son of Nicholas Coulburn and Eliz. His Wife, of the Parish, gent., but late of Watford in the County of Hertford ... his father, Peter Coulburn, gent., both deceased & together entombed at Watford aforesaid whose ... ancestors were formerly of Lancashire. The first named Nicholas the youngest, departed this life in the 20th day of April A.D. 1737, aged

& [was] buried at Barking. The Waldron family resided in this Parish for generations. Christopher Waldron purchased the Ilford Hospital Estate of a Mrs Thrale, whose daughter he married & this lady in 1719 rebuilt the Almshouses attached & had other improvements made there. In 1739 the Waldron family disposed of this Estate. The Barking section of this family possessed & resided in North Street & in 1894 finally sold their property & house, the site of which is now occupied by the North Street Schools.

1789. Waldron, Roger of Barking Parish – Citizen & Draper of London.

1824. Waldron, John of Barking Parish – Citizen & Draper of London.

1815. Waldron, Elizabeth, wife of above said John Waldron[160].

1705. Pittman, Mary. Age 30. Wife of Thomas Pittman of Ilford.

1751. Pittman, Ann. Second wife of above Thomas. Died 5th March[161].

1760. Pittman, Thomas. Husband of above Mary & Anne. Died 17th January. Age 89.

1791 Pittman, Thomas, of Loxford Hall, Feb [?], also his wife[162].

1800. Pittman, William, died January 1800. Age 20.

1818. Pittman, Thomas, of Loxford Hall. Feb 18th. Also his wife. His age 27[163].

1821. Pittman, Susanna, of Loxford Hall. Age 27.

1813. Pittman, William, brother to Thomas (1818), also his wife Elizabeth,

---

17 years and – months. "Whom God loves dearly, He oft calls early". Also Nicholas Coulburn of this Parish, gent., Father of the above Nicholas Coulburn, who died April 27th 1739 in the 66th year of his Age ... Elizabeth Walrond ... the Wife of the above Nicholas Coulburn, who departed this life ... in the 66th year of her Age". On the north panel of the tomb: "John Walrond Esq., late of this Parish, who died at Ilford on the 20th day of January, 1863, in the 78th year of his Age".

160 She died on 1st September 1815, aged 24.

161 According to the 1930 register, Ann Pittman died in 1751, aged 68.

162 According to the 1930 survey, Thomas Pittman of Loxford died on 21st February 1791, and gives his age as 18, which must be an error; nor does it mention his wife, another Mary.

163 According to the 1930 register, this Thomas Pittman died on 17th February 1818, aged 49. Susanna Pittman, his widow, died on 21st January 1820, aged 62. His son Thomas died on 14th September 1818, aged 27. Also mentioned in the register is William Pittman, who died on 14th December 1813, aged 16. He was not married and the wife

who pre-deceased him.

This enterprising family of Farmers resided at Loxford Hall, where an account is given of them[164]. Elizabeth, daughter of Thomas (1791) married Thomas Newman of Eastbury House & he died in 1792[165]. Also see "Agriculture" for a notice of this family, who was famous for their potato crops. There are several other members of this family, who were buried in Barking Churchyard.

1728. Skinner, Katherine, wife of Ambrose Skinner.

1778. Skinner, Ambrose, of Longbridge Farm.

1780. Skinner, William, & Sarah his wife.

1781. Skinner, Ambrose.

1789. Skinner, Ann, wife of Ambrose (1778).

1789. Skinner, Thomas, of Aldersbrooke, Little Ilford.

1819. Skinner, Thomas, of Aldersbrooke, Little Ilford. Son.

This was also a successful family of Farmers, for which Barking Parish could well boast of at that period[166].

1779. Lynall, Thomas.

1781. Lynall, Ann, wife of Thomas (1779).

1792. Lynall, Lydia, daughter of above.

Some of this family resided at Little Ilford, at which churchyard is a Tomb in memory of Thomas Lynall who died 1815 & his wife in 1828.

Elizabeth referred to by Frogley might be a sister or an aunt. The 1930 register also includes the grave of Elizabeth, wife of the William Pittman who farmed Loxford in the 18th century, and this could be the source of the confusion.

164 "During most, if not all, of the 18th century, Loxford was leased to the Pittman family". *VCH Essex: vol.5.* p.206.

165 The upper part of this headstone was indecipherable by 1930. Two later inscriptions for a Mrs Elizabeth Newman were readable, one dated 1810, the other 1830.

166 See *Barking vestry minutes.* 1955. p.325.

1761. Hunsdon, Jonas, of Bennetts Castle[167].

1781. Hunsdon, James, of Bennetts Castle[168].

1781. Hunsdon, Mary, wife of James (1781). Age. 36.

1814. Hunsdon, James, of Bennetts Castle.

1815. Hunsdon, Katherine, wife of James (1814). Age 75.

This family of farmers was very numerous in the Parish, possessing Downshall, Uphall, &c. Henry Hunsdon possessed Uphall-Farm[169]: James Hunsdon resided at the Manor Farm, Little Ilford[170] & who died 1855 & his wife 1877, both buried in Little Ilford Churchyard, where there are other monuments to this family.

1758. Parsons, John[171]. [Page 123]

1763. Parsons, Jane, wife of John (1758).

1766. Parsons, Samuel, child of John & Jane Parsons.

1780. Parsons, Ann, child of John & Jane Parsons.

1800. Parsons, William.

1833. Parsons, Rebecca, wife of William (1800).

I am informed that this family is not connected with the "Parson" family, that for about a century was Landlords of the "Bull Inn"[172].

1774. Heath, Mrs Frances. Age 72[173].

---

167 Jonas Hunsdon, Surveyor, Chadwell, 1749; Overseer, 1755. *Barking vestry minutes.* 1955. p.321.

168 See *Barking vestry minutes.* 1955. p.321 for more than one James Hunsdon.

169 Most likely as a tenant rather than as owner. See: *VCH Essex: Vol.5.* p.211.

170 James Hunsdon, farmer, Aldborough Hatch. (White 1848).

171According to the 1930 register, John Parsons, senior, died in May 1758, aged 56. John Parsons, junior, died in August 1756, aged 30.

172 Members of the Parsons family were farming Bennetts Castle before the Hunsdons and continued to farm in the Goodmayes area later in the 18th century. A James Parsons was still tenant of Ravenings in the early 19th century and a William Parsons was farming in the Barkingside area in 1855 (Kelly's). For the Parsons family, landlords of the Bull Inn, see *Mr Frogley's Barking: a first selection.* 2002. p.34.

173 The 1930 register gives Mr Francis Heath of Barking, who died 30th June 1772, aged 72.

1786. Meredith, Thomas, of Gaysham Hall[174].

1787. Meredith, Sarah, wife of Thomas.

1756. Vaughan, Roger, a Brandy Merchant of Barking & a very wealthy man[175]. He was possessed of much land in the town & which is now very valuable, but wether the rightful owners are enjoying it is very doubtful. He was a descendant of Roger Vaughan, who in 1656 was a Surgeon-Barber, and resided at Barking. Vaughan, Roger [1756] was a wealthy Brandy Merchant & a descendant of Roger Vaughan of Barking, who in 1656 was a Surgeon Barber. In reference to the son (1756) the writer is almost pursuaded to mention fully – as conveyed to him from genuine sources – the mysterious manner in which Mr Vaughans extensive property in Barking is now possessed by people who has no legal right to it. I make this assertion & although difficult to prove still remains a fact. One thing I am convinced of is that their claims will not bear honest investigation.

1767. Day, Daniel – Originator of Fairlop Fair[176].

---

174 "In 1733 Gayshams was on lease to Thomas Meredith, whose son of the same name was tenant until 1781 or later". *VCH Essex: Vol.5*. p.205. See *Barking vestry minutes*. 1955. p.323 for this family. According to the 1930 register, Thomas died on 31 July 1786, aged 63; his wife Sarah died on 15 September 1787, aged 59.

175 Frogley duplicates this entry. The two paragraphs on Roger Vaughan have been combined here.

176 Frogley writes about Daniel Day on page 9 of the manuscript, with an illustration of his tombstone in Barking churchyard: "Daniel Day was born at St Marys, Overy in 1682, and eventually was in business of a "Block & Pump maker" at Wapping. He also possessed a small Estate in Essex, & which he visited annually – near the Forest. In this Forest was an immense Oak tree and it stood near to the present "Maypole Inn" at Barkingside. Annually he visited this spot & later invited friends to join him there, & so the company increased so that he lived to see a regular Fair with booths &c. His company consisted of 30 or 40 in [h]is own trade, who went down in a boat – cut from an entire fir – with an awning & mounted on a carriage drawn by 6 horses. He died on Oct 19th 1767 Aged 84 & his body was placed in a coffin cut out from a "limb" of this tree previous to his death, & [was] conveyed to Barking Churchyard by water in compliance with his wishes. His mourners included 6 journeymen pump-masters to whom he bequeathed a new leather apron & a guinea. In 1793 this tree was fenced in & in June 1805 whilst some visitors injured the tree by a fire they had under it & in Feb 1820 a storm destroyed it. The Fair – every 1st Friday in July – is now of the past, although a Boat – as above – went annually up to about 1880. The Pulpit of St Pancras Church was made from this Oak". The 1930 register refers to Daniel Day, late of St John's Wapping, died 19 October 1767, aged 84.

1670. More, Thomas[177]. This Memorial is built or attached to the East-Wall of the Church & the Epitaph is very curious as below. Mr More was a Churchwarden & resided at Eastbury House – his Coat of Arms still remains in the House. On the heading of the Memorial is:- Here lyeth ye body of Thomas More, who departed this life, April ye 6th 1670, being then Churchwarden of this Parish.

Epitaph referred to:

"Stay here awhile, his sad fate deplore

Here lyes the body of one Thomas More.

His name was More, but now it may be said

He is no more, because that now he's dead

And in this place doth lye sepulchered".

1728. Nepton, Ann.

1724. Nepton, Thomas, of Ilford. They were great benefactors to the Poor of Barking & Harglatte (in his Livery Companies) give the particulars of this Legacy & which is written at the foot of this note.

EPHITAPH

Beneath this Tomb are deposited the Remains of Mr Thomas Nepton formerly of this Parish, who departed this life on the 26th day of September 1724 in the 49th year of his age.

Also of
Mrs Ann Nepton wife of the above, who departed this life on the 2nd day of May 1728 in the 64th year of her age.
This Tomb was repaired & beautified in the year 1825
by an Order of the Court of

---

177 Frogley provides the following footnote regarding the More family on page 420 of the manuscript, as part of the section dealing with Eastbury House: "This family appears to have originated from Cheshire, but some of them resided in Barking, Dagenham & Orsett, Essex. Thomas More of Eastbury House [was] married at Dagenham to Joanna Summers & it was probably that Thomas More, to whom the following Epitaph was inscribed to upon a slab on the East-Wall of Barking Church, in the Church-Yard. His Coat of Arms is in the room over the Great Hall in Eastbury". According to the 1930 register, More was 35 when he died.

Assistants of the Worshipful Company of Poulterers, London made on the 31st day of March in the same year to which Company the above named Thomas and Ann Nepton gave & devised considerable Estates in Trust for Charitable purposes.

Note: "The greater part of the Revenues of the Poulterers Coy of whom Mr Thomas Nepton was a member, was derived from dividends in respect of £11,899 paid by the Great Eastern & North London Railways for compulsory purchase of Freeholds in Dumming Alley, Bishopsgate & from which they received about £500 a year. The Company acquired the property under the Will of Thomas Nepton, dated 6th May 1718, subject to certain Trusts which on the death of his wife Anne in 1728 a payment was charged of £40 to the Poor of Barking & the like to St Botolphs Aldgate & about £20 to the Shoreditch School. The residue was then divisible between the Poor of the Guild & Apprenticeship Fees. The Copy of the Indenture, painted up at Barking Church, bequeathed, after the death of Joseph Green, all her Estate in Bishopsgate to the Poulterers Coy & the same was invested by them upon Trust in 1764 … to be paid by two half yearly payments as follows:

£20 on January 26th and £20 on July 26th. [?]

For further particulars of this handsome Legacy see "Charities".

1781. Leigh, Ann.

1826. Glenny, William, son of William who married Molly Sibley.

1828. Glenny, Elizabeth. Age 27.

1838. Glenny, Sarah. Age 62. Sisters, and Aunts to William (1826).

1833. Glenny, Deborah.

1839. Glenny, Henry. Brother to William (1826).

1839. Glenny, George. Age 67. Brother to Sarah & Elizabeth (above).

1843. Glenny, Alexander. Age 43[178]. Brother to George (1838).

1850. Glenny, William. Age 81. Brother to Alexander.

1850. Glenny, Kate Wallis. Grandaughter of William (1850).

---

178 According to the 1930 register, Alexander was 78 when he died. It is curious that Frogley fails to notice the earlier grave, which commemorates the founders of the Barking dynasty – Alexander Glenny (d.1782) and his wife Deborah (d.1804) - until later in this list.

1856. Glenny, Mary, Miss. Age 83. Probably sister of William (1850).

1830. Sibley, Sarah. Mother-in-Law of William (1826).

1844. Foulkes, Sarah, wife of Thomas Foulkes of Barkingside[179].

1828. Frogley, Elizabeth[180], wife of Joseph Frogley[181].

1864. Frogley, Joseph[182], son of above Joseph Frogley. Ancestors of the Writer.

1817. Plows, Richard.

1884. Plows, Mary.

1886. Plows, Harry, son of Mary.

1853. Goodaker, William. Age 27.

1877. Goodaker, Henry, father of William (1853)[183].

1898. Goodaker, Catherine, wife of Henry (1877). Age 98.

1878. Weatherall, James. Age 90[184]. This – a short stout man – was a purveyor of oil-skins &c then used by the Fishermen & [from] which he amassed money. He resided in a small shop in Heath Street at the corner of a Court named Weatheralls Court. He was a benefactor to the town (see Charities)[185]. He had an housekeeper who in her later years resided in the almshouses. Her name was Rebecca Balsham. She was buried in his grave. (See next item).

1881. Lester, Rebekah – know as Rebekah Balsham. Age 66.

---

179 Thomas Foulkes, gentleman, Barkingside. (White 1848).

180 Elizabeth Moungall, born c.1767, who married Joseph Frogley in 1788. According to Geoffrey Frogley, Elizabeth died on 7 October 1823, and not 1828 as in Frogley's manuscript or 1829 as in the 1930 register of graves.

181 Joseph Frogley (1765-1847), fisherman and landlord of the Blue Anchor. Great-grandfather of William Holmes Frogley.

182 Joseph Frogley (1789-1864), fisherman, grandfather of William Holmes Frogley. Joseph married Ann Doous (d.1836) in 1815.

183 Henry Goodacre, wheelwright, North Street. (White's 1848); Henry Goodaker, wheelwright, North Street. (Kelly's 1871).

184 James Wetherall, Surveyor, Barking, 1833, 1856. *Barking vestry minutes.* 1955. p.326. James Wetherill, tailor and slopseller, Heath Street. (Pigot 1839, White 1848). Date of death given as 1879 in the 1930 register.

185 "James Wetherill, by will proved 1879, gave £100 stock to relieve poor fishermen or their wives and children with sums of 2s". *VCH Essex: Vol.5.* p.235.

1906. Lester, John James. Aged 92.

1806. Oldaker, Rebecca. Also several children.

1808. Oldaker, Kinmill, husband of Rebecca, of Gayshams Hall.

1823. Oldaker, Caroline, daughter of Thomas & Elizabeth of Gayshams Hall.

1807. Allen, Ann. Wife of Poulton Allen & daughter of John Cocking, Surveyor of Barking.

1878. Peacock, Frederick Francis, of Longbridge Farm.

1849. Grout, Joseph (Sept). Shipsmith & small smack-owner[186].

1812. Marchant, George[187].

1811. Marchant, James, son of George (1812)[188].

1822. Marchant, George, son of George (1812)[189].

1861. Marchant, Elizabeth.

1882. Marchant, Henry. Father of Elizabeth (1861).

1889. Marchant, Susan. Mother of Elizabeth (1861).

1877. Marchant, Susannah.

1895. Marchant, William[190], husband of Susannah (1877) & brother of Henry (1882).

Henry Marchant (1882) [was] formerly a Smackowner[191] & later a Salesman at Barking Gates. He was medium height, stout & very affable & jocular. He was a member of the Wesleyans & resided at Northbury House, Tanner

---

186 Joseph Grout, blacksmith & shipsmith. (Pigot 1839, White's 1848).

187 "Unfortunately lost at sea, 27 Oct 1812, age 35", according the 1930 register.

188 "Unfortunately drowned, 2 Aug 1811, age 4yrs 3 ms", according to the 1930 register.

189 "Who was lost at sea, 4 Dec 1826, age 22", according to the 1930 register. These first three tragic Marchant burials are recorded on a panel of the family tomb of the Morgan family – presumably the families were related.

190 William Marchant, Vicarage Villa, Axe Street. (Kelly's 1890).

191 Hannibal, Henry and William Merchant, smack owners. (Kelly's 1851).

Street[192]. The loss of his daughter Elizabeth was a great trouble to her parents. William, brother of Henry, was also a Smackowner, but for many years led a retired life – residing on his property Vicarage Cottages, Axe Street[193].

1855. Morgan, Elizbeth. Age 70.

1858. Morgan, James, Husband of Elizbeth[194].

1865. Morgan, James[195].

1895. Morgan, Mary Ann[196], wife of James (1865).

This was also a family of Smackowners, but the most successful one was James (1865) who rose from a cabin boy to owner & after his death was worth many Thousands of pounds. He built Fawley House, East Street. His wife Mary Ann died at Sydenham (in Bromley) Kent. Their eldest daughter married Mr Ashmole in 1863 of the "Angel Inn" Ilford[197]. James, Eldest son of Mary Ann, resided in Chesnut House, Tanner Street. He was a Smackowner & although his father left so much money & to a good going business, the son eventually failed & [has] since died.

1820. Glover, Sarah.

1821. Glover, Rev Richard[198].

---

192 Henry Marchant's Northbury House stood on the corner of Tanner Street and Hart Street, facing south down North Street. It is to be distinguished from the Northbury House in North Street, the former old vicarage house, which was later owned by the Quash family. For further information regarding the Marchant family, see *Mr Frogley's Barking: a first selection*. 2002. p.98.

193 Vicarage Cottages stood on the northwest corner of Axe Street and Ripple Road (OS 25-inch map, 1862). The 1841 census records Henry Marchant living in the first of them with his wife, a servant and four apprentices. See also *Mr Frogley's Barking: a first selection*. 2002. p.98.

194 James Morgan, smack owner. (Kelly's 1851).

195 According to the 1930 register, James Thomas Morgan died in 1865, aged 41. His wife Mary Ann died in 1895, aged 79. According to the 1861 census, James and Mary Ann were then accommodating 20 apprentices, mainly London poor-law apprentices, in their two houses in Heath Street. The widow Mary Ann sold all the 29 remaining ships of the Gamecock fleet to Robert Hewett in 1868.

196 Mrs Morgan, Fawley House, East Street. (Kelly's 1890).

197 William Ashmole, Angel, Ilford. (Pigot 1839); Henry Jubilee Ashmole, Angel Inn (posting & excise & stamp office). (White 1848).

198 The Revd Richard Glover was instituted as Vicar of Dagenham in 1811 but was appointed acting Chaplain of Ilford Hospital Chapel in 1814. He offered his resignation

Husband & Wife. He took the services at Ilford Hospital on Sunday, on behalf of the Chaplain, who was residing at Islington. This was evidently an old Barking family, as a William Glover died at Barking in 1660 & was a Yeoman of His Majestys Guard.

1870. Manby, Ann, wife of Dr Manby.

1877. Manby, Dr John M.D. of Barking.

Dr Manby resided at Westbury House, Barking[199]. He died at Teddington Middlesex & [was] buried at Barking. (See Westbury).

1879. Budd, William. Agent for an Insurance Co., but later for many years was a Pawnbroker in the Broadway[200].

1864. Hobday, Elgar[201].

1874. Hobday, Sarah[202].

Husband & wife. They were tallow-chandlers & made all the "Dips" or candles that was used in the district. Their shop was in Axe Street. (See Axe Street).

1847. Kincey, Josiah.

1857. Kincey, Mary[203].

Husband & Wife. They [were] market gardeners & farmers on a small scale. Their son had the farm now the site of Victoria Road to the Railway & from

---

from Dagenham since he preferred to live at Ilford, but his patron persuaded him to continue as Vicar until 1816. At Ilford he acted for the Revd Bennet Allen who lived at Islington. Bennet Allen died in 1819 and was succeeded by the more zealous Oliver Lodge, Curate in Charge of St Margaret's, Barking, though he may have continued to use the services of Glover for a while. The Revd Richard Glover, who was born in Westmoreland, died in January 1824. There is no reason to connect him with the earlier Barking family, as Frogley suggests.

199 Should be Manley. John Manley bought Westbury House from J. S. Thompson in 1843. *VCH Essex: vol.5*. p.213. John Manley, M.D., Westbury. (Kelly's 1851).

200 William Budd, agent to Defender Insurance Company, High Street. (Kelly's 1851).

201 Edgar Hobday, tallow chandler, Axe Street. (Pigot 1839, White's 1848). The 1930 register of graves gives the year of his death as 1867, but the burial register confirms Frogley's date of August 1864.

202 Sarah S. Hobday, aged 43, in East of London Family History *Society 1851 census index series: vol.1, part 4*. 1984. p.18.

203 Kincey and Kinsey in: East of London Family History *Society 1851 census index series: vol.1, part 4*. 1984. p.20.

the Roding to Ilford Lane.

1837. Dangerfield, Sarah.

1846. Dangerfield, James.

Husband & Wife. An old Barking family. A row of Cottages in North Street is called Dangerfield Cottages. Also the peice of vacant land at [the] corner of Cow-Lane & North Street was their property.

1848. Dangerfield, Jane.

1870. Munday, Mary Ann.

Two daughters of Sarah & James.

1831. Forge[204], Sarah, died April 8th[205].

[Page 127]

1843. Forge, Richard W. January 11th. Husband of above Sarah[206].

1858. Forge, Elizbeth. June.

1861. Forge, Richard. April[207]. Smackowner, and parents of the above Sarah & Richard Walrond Forge.

1849. Forge, Mary.

1883. Forge, John. Late sailmaker & smackowner[208].

1879. Forge, Elizbeth, wife of Thomas Forge (1892).

1892. Forge, Thomas. Watchmaker & Newsagent. (See North Street)[209].

---

204 For Forge family see East of London Family History Society *1851 census index series: vol.1, part 4*: Essex: Barking. 1984. p.13-14. Also *Mr Frogley's Barking: a first selection*. 2002. p.97.

205 The 1930 register of graves gives Sarah Forge's year of death as 1821, but St Margaret's burial register confirms Frogley – she died in April 1831.

206 According to the 1930 register, Richard Walrond Forge was the brother, not the husband, of Sarah. According to St Margaret's burial register, he died at Mile End Old Town in January 1843, aged 28.

207 St Margaret's burial register shows that Richard Forge was buried on 17th November 1861, aged 83.

208 St Margaret's burial register does not list John Forge who died in 1883, but Kelly's 1855 lists a John Forge, smackowner and sailmaker, in Fisher Street. Later in this list, Frogley notices an earlier John Forge who died in 1833.

209 Thomas Forge, watch maker & draper, Broadway. (Kelly's 1878). The 1841 census shows the 18 years old Thomas Forge apprenticed to Daniel Mathias, watchmaker, in North Street. For further information regarding Thomas Forge, see *Mr Frogley's Barking: a first selection*. 2002. p.37.

His only son Thomas Forge who kept on the Watchmaking business some time at length became a Postman at Ilford for 20 years. Died January 1912 & buried at City of London Cemetery.

1875. Hawes, Daniel, formerly of Queens Road. Farmer[210]. He died at Hawthorne Terrace, which he built. His widow later married Albert Chalk, Station-master at Barking & later at Southend.

1904. Chalk, Albert, late Station-master at Barking[211] – having succeeded his father. By his marriage with Mrs Hawes he became possessed of Hawthorne Terrace. He was transferred as Station-Master to Southend, where he died in Oct 1904. His wife predeceased him in December 1885.

1809. Burrell, Mary (Sept.)[212]

1840. Burrell, George (May).

1853. Burrell, Mary, wife of George[213].

1874. Burrell, George Augustus, Aug 11[214].

George Augustus was a Farmer, and also had Hay, Straw & Coal wharves at Barking Creek[215]. He resided at the Chesnut House, Tanner Street, recently demolished for Railway Extension. He at one time acted as Surveyor of Barking under the Old Urban Authority.

1861. Holmes, Mary[216].

1862. Holmes, Jeremiah. Wife[217] of Mary (see Axe Street).

---

210 Daniel Hawes, market gardener, Rippleside. (Kelly's 1871).

211 Albert Chalk, station master, East Street. (Kelly's 1890).

212 The 1930 register of graves and St Margaret's burial register agree that she died in September 1810, aged 73, and not 1809.

213 Mary A. Burrell, aged 70, in: East of London Family History Society *1851 census index series: vol.1, part 4.* 1984. p.7.

214 George Augustus Burrell, Surveyor, Barking, 1854-67; Churchwarden, 1859-67. *Barking vestry minutes.* 1955. p. 318. Coal, corn & lime merchant, East Street & Tanner Street, & at Ilford wharf, High Street, Great Ilford. (Kelly's 1871).

215 Burrells Wharf was put up for sale in 1873. There was also a store in Broadway known as "Mr Burrells Farmyard" which was acquired by his manager, Edward Deveson.

216 Mary Holmes, aged 63, in: East of London Family History *Society 1851 census index series: vol.1, part 4.* 1984. p.19. The 1930 register of graves in St Margaret's churchyard and the burial register give the date of her death as 1866, not 1861.

217 Husband.

Also known as William[218].

1868. Holmes, William. Son of Jeremiah. He kept & died at the Cock Inn, East Ham[219].

1865. Holmes, Sarah Garad (Oct 21). 1st wife of James Holmes (1881).

1881. Holmes, James. (See the George Inn)[220].

1893. Holmes, Mary[221]. 2nd wife of above James Holmes. Died 2d Dec 1893 Aged 57. After her husbands death she kept on the business at the "George" & eventually greatly increased the business in consequence of the building on the Byfrons Estate. Her death terminated the Holmes' tenancy of the George, after over 40 years.

1834. Winmill, Ann[222]. A descendant of the Winmill family who possessed the Farm of Valence in 1814. This old moated manor house was in Dagenham Parish.

1896. Jackson, Daniel T.[223] A successful contractor (cartage). See East Street.

1783. Horsley, John. (March) [Page 128]

1814. Horsley, Susannah (Dec), wife of John (1783).

1844. Horsley, James (Jany)[224] (and)

1832. Horsley, John. Sons of above John & Susannah.

1871. Horsley, William (Aug)[225].

1879. Horsley, Sarah (Dec)

1848. Ringer, John[226].

---

218 William Holmes, bricklayer, Axe Street. (Pigot 1839, White 1848, Kelly's 1851). St Margaret's burial register says he died in 1867, aged 82.

219 St Margaret's burial register gives date of death as 21st March 1869, and abode as West Ham.

220 James Holmes, George, & auctioneer, surveyor & appraiser, Broadway. (Kelly's 1871).

221 Mrs Mary Ann Holmes, George Hotel, Broadway. (Kelly's 1890).

222 The daughter of William and Ann Parsons.

223 Daniel Thomas Jackson, grocer, 83 Axe Street. (Kelly's 1890).

224 According to the 1930 register of graves and St Margaret's burial register, James Horsley was grandson, not son, of John and Susannah Horsley, and died in December 1815, aged 16.

225 William Horsley, mast, oar & block maker, smack owner & pump borer. (Kelly's 1851).

226 John Ringer, Still, Fisher Street. (White's 1848).

Some of this family kept the "Still" now called the Barking Cross Tavern, & was related to the "Ringer" family, who also had the house. (See the Still[227]). William was a mast & block maker & smack owner & his brother Luke kept the "Still" in Fisher Street[228].

1877. Ringer, Rebecca[229], of the Still, but after a retired life for many years, died at her residence in Queens Road & near her resided Mr Horsley whom I believe chiefly depended upon her for his support.

1812. Harris, John (Sept)[230].

1837. Harris, Elizbeth, wife of John.

1849. Harris, John, son of above, a Smackowner.

1864. Harris, Thomas, Sailmaker & ships-chandler[231].

There are several more of this family buried here. They were Smackowners[232], Sailmakers, Ships-Chandlers, Grocers &c. Three of the family at the same time possessed Smacks.

1825. Mead, John. Farmer. Age 78[233].

1814. Mead, Ann, wife of John (1825).

---

227 Later known as Barking Cross Tavern. See *Mr Frogley's Barking: a first selection*. 2002. p.53-54.

228 Luke Horsley, smack owner, Fisher Street. (White's 1848); Still, Fisher Street. (Kelly's 1851).

229 Rebecca Belchand (Belcham), Fisher Street. (Pigot 1839); Mrs Ringer, North Street. (Kelly's 1851). Mrs Ringer, aged 77 when she died, was William Horsley's sister.

230 According to the 1930 register, John Harris, sailmaker, died in September 1812, aged 61.

231 Thomas Harris, sailmaker, ship chandler & agent to the County Fire & Provident Life office. (Kelly's 1851). The 1930 register of graves and St Margaret's burial register agree he died in July 1854, aged 69, not 1864. In the 1840s and 1850s Thomas Harris was living in a house in Broadway immediately north of the Congregational Church belonging to the Hewetts (Tithe award 1847 and 1851 census). His sail-loft stood on Hewett's wharf. The house later became a draper's shop owned by Willetts.

232 Mrs Harris, smack owner; Joseph Harris, smack owner, Bull Street; John Harris, smack owner, Axe Street. (Kelly's 1851). Rebecca Harris of Roden Lodge is described as a smackowner in the 1841 census, and four 15 year old apprentices were also living there.

233 This John Mead was tenant of a farm in Barley Lane later known as Blue House Farm, which eventually, at the end of the 19th century, became the site of Goodmayes Mental Hospital.

1852. Mead, John, son of above John & Ann[234].

1875. Mead, Elizbeth. Wife of John (1852).

1848. Milton, Joseph (May). Age 35.

1880. Milton, Louisa. (Wife of Joseph).

1874. Milton, Frederick.

Joseph died at the Rose & Crown, Fisher Street[235] & Louisa, his wife, died at Gorleston, Age 67. Their son Fredk died at the Rose & Crown, through an illness caused by wading in the water, during a flood from the Roding. He was formerly a Chorister at the Church, possessing a fine Bass voice, but by the introduction of a surpliced choir, he left the Church & attended the Congregational body.

1865. Patch, William (Feb).

1882. Patch, Mary Elizbeth, wife of William (1865).

1888. Patch, Sarah, sister of Thomas. She died at Folkestone, Sept 1888 & [is] buried at Barking.

1887. Patch, Thomas. Age 79, of Fair-Cross Farm. (See Fair Cross Farm)[236].

1810. Stanley, William[237].

1819. Stanley, Margaret (Wife of above).

In this Tomb is also buried some of the Lake family. The Stanley family resided in Stanley House, Heath Street, now pulled down.

1837. Lake, Richard[238]

1856. Lake, John.

Buried in the Stanley Tomb & relatives of that family. John was a small Smackowner, Shoemaker & Grocers in the Broadway[239].

---

234 John Mead, gentleman, Ilford Lane. (White 1848).

235 For the Milton family and the Rose & Crown see *Mr Frogley's Barking: a first selection*. 2002. p.54.

236 Thomas Patch, market gardener, Faircross, East Street. (Kelly's 1878).

237 The 1930 register of graves says that William Tarr Stanley died in August 1814, not 1810. However, he does not appear in St Margaret's burial register for either year!

238 The 1930 register of graves says he died in 1857, not 1837, but there is no entry in St Margaret's burial register to confirm either date.

239 John Lake, smack owner, High Street. (White's 1848); smack owner, shoemaker & grocer, High Street. (Kelly's 1851).

The inaugural meeting of St John's Ambulance at Upney Isolation Hospital in 1907. Dr Fenton is in the centre. (See pages 52 - 53).

89

Joshua King, Headmaster of the National Schools.(See pages 107 - 108).

Longbridge Farm and Barking boundary posts at the foot of Goodmayes Lane. (See pages 16 and 25).

Painting of Manor Farm. (See pages 15 - 16).

EDWARD DEVESON

(31 years Manager to the late

G. O. AUG. BURRELL, Esq.,

Corn and Coal Merchant,

FISHER STREET, BARKING),

BEGS to announce to the Gentry and Inhabitants of Barking and surrounding neighbourhood, that he has TAKEN THE PREMISES, known as

MR. BURRELL'S FARM YARD,

Situate in the

BROADWAY, BARKING,

Opposite the George Inn,

Where he has opened a Depôt for the Sale of Corn, Coal, and Coke, Oil and Cotton Cakes, Hay and Straw, at Wholesale and Retail Prices, and hopes by strict attention to business to merit the support and patronage so liberally bestowed upon the late Firm.

Barking, Oct. 1874.

(See pages 85 & 112).

The Revd. Paul Thomas with officers of the Poulterers Company, who distribute the Nepton charity. Photograph taken in 1991 (See pages 78 - 79).

Bamford's watercolour of Northbury House, the former vicarage, painted in 1905. (See footnote 192)

OLD LEVEL CROSSING, BARKING.

East Street level crossing, looking east. (See page 12).

Oilette postcard of Barking Park gates. Note the early car - George Wilmott Glenny was the first Barking car owner in 1904.

Children sketching at the 18th century graves of the Parsons family in St Margaret's churchyard.

Frogley's picture of the pond in Ripple Road. Pages 402 - 403 in the manuscript. (See also page 127)

Frogley's drawing of the Presbytery, on page 293 of the manuscript. (See page 139).

Page 290 in the manuscript.

Page 297 in the manuscript - Frogley's drawing of the Friends meeting house in North Street. (See page 142).

The Revd. George Corney and his wife. (See page 136).

Ripple Castle, built 1811 - 1814 by Thomas Tyser. (See page 39).

1873. Lake, John (son of John 1856)[240]. Shoemaker & Church Beadle[241]. He was the last liveried Beadle at Barking Church.

1884. Lake, Elizabeth, wife of John (1873).

1895. Lake, William, son of John & Elizbeth[242]. He succeeded his father in the shoemakers business, situate on the corner, opposite the Bull Inn. After the formation of the Local Board he was appointed Rate Collector.

1845. Bellis, Hugh (May)[243].

1866. Bellis, Augustus (Oct).

They were Tobacco pipe manufacturers in the Barking Road & after their deaths Mrs Penelope – wife of Hugh – continued the business[244].

1860. Linsdell, Mary,

1878. Linsdell, Thomas[245].

Husband & wife, of the Ship Inn, Heath Street (See "Ship").

---

240 Aged 72 when he died in 1873.

241 On page 77 of the manuscript, Frogley adds the following footnote: "John Lake was a short stout man, and had a shoemakers shop at the corner of East St, opposite the Bull Inn. With his long cane he was a terror to the boys in the Church. He died in May 1873 & his wife Elizbeth in 1884 – both [are] buried in the Churchyard. His son succeeded him as Sexton but wore no livery, but the office was soon abolished here. This son William Lake was also a Shoemaker, but after the formation of the Local Board he was appointed Poor Rate Collector, which he retained until his death in 1895. He then resided in a house in the Longbridge Rd, since pulled down by the recent Railway Improvement".

242 William Lake, house agent & collector to Local Board, Longbridge Road. (Kelly's 1890). On page 253 of the manuscript, Frogley writes: "Collector of Rates – Mr William Lake. Formerly a shoemaker & succeeded his father as the "Parish Beadle". His duties was to collect all rates & monies due to his Board. He received a Commission of [2.5] per cent upon rates received from parties assessed at less than £1000 rateable value & 1 per cent at those assessed at £1000 and over".

243 Hugh Bellis, tobacco pipe maker. (Kelly's 1845).

244 Mrs Bellis, pipe maker. (White's 1848); Mrs Penelope Bellis, tobacco pipe maker. (Kelly's 1851).

245 Thomas Linsdell, Ship Inn, Heath Street. (Kelly's 1851). He was aged 85 at the time of his death. See also *Mr Frogley's Barking: a first selection*. 2002. p.73.

1858. Lambert, John. Age 57. A farmer & resided in the Broadway[246].

1809. Lambert, John. Father of above. Several more of this family is buried here.

1862. Gibbard, Esther Ann (Feb)[247].

1881. Gibbard, Charles Lewis (Jany)[248].

1855. Scrimes, John. A ship & boat builder of Fisher Street[249].

1814. Hewett, Sarah[250], wife of:

1850. Hewett, Scrymgeour[251].& four of their children.

1841. Hewett, Ann, wife of:

1871. Hewett, Samuel.& five of their infant children.

1890. Hewett, Clarissa Hannah, died March 1890 – 2nd wife of Thomas[252] who died 1871 & step-mother to Mr Robert Hewett of Roden Lodge[253]. She died at York Lodge, Erith, Age 81.

---

246 Despite various addresses given in trade directories for John Matthews Lambert – for example, John Lambert, farmer, North Street. (White's 1848) – his residence would appear from the Tithe Award and the 1851 census to have been Tanners Farm, which stood on the corner of Tanner Street and Harts Lane opposite the north end of North Street (nowadays this end of Tanner Street is also named North Street). In the 1841 census this was the residence of a John Lambert and his wife, Martha. Following the latter's death, this became the site of Henry Marchant's Northbury House. The farm had little adjacent land, but the Lamberts were market gardeners or graziers and the 180 acres occupied in 1851 lay in scattered parcels.

247 Esther Ann Gibbard, grocer & beer retailer, Manor Road, listed in Kelly's 1871 and 1878 was presumably a relative. See also *Mr Frogley's Barking: a first selection*. 2002. p.150.

248 According to the 1930 register, he was "husband of the above" Esther Ann Gibbard. For the shops tenanted by the Gibbards see *Mr Frogley's Barking: a first selection*. 2002. p.150.

249 John Scrimes, blacksmith, Fisher Street. (Pigot 1839); shipwright, Fisher Street. (White's 1848); ship & boat builder, Fisher Street. (Kelly's 1851).

250 St Margaret's burial register confirms she died in 1814, although the 1930 register of graves says 1811.

251 Scrymgeour was aged 84 when he died in 1850.

252 Clarissa Hewett was the second wife of Samuel, not Thomas, Hewett, who died in 1871. Thomas, Samuel's youngest brother, never married. He was looked after by a housekeeper and is thought to have been mentally retarded. Thomas was buried on 13th November 1861, aged 56.

253 Robert Hewett, iron ship builder, Roding Yard, West Bank; Robert Hewett & Co., steam ship owners, Fisher Street. (Kelly's 1890).

(Date obliterated on tomb). Taylor, Henry Vere. Capt 3rd Essex Artillery. The writer saw this funeral (about 186?) with full Military honours. He was an M.D. & highly respected[254]. The Foresters Society also attended in their full strength, in fact, such a procession has not been seen since in the town.

1858. Pearson, Sarah. [Page 130]

1863. Pearson, William

1863. Pearson, Louisa.

1882. Pearson, James.

1885. Pearson, Sarah Ann.

1893. Pearson, James.

James (1882) & Sarah Ann (1885) was parents of the other three – The two first dying very young. This family has resided in Barking many years as Butchers. James (1882) had originally a shop in Trafalgar Place[255] & his brother John was Butcher & Smackowner in the Broadway[256] & to which James succeeded. Dying in 1882 his son James managed the business with his sister. This James was a batchelor & retiring from business, shortly afterwards visited Chicago America, to see the Exhibition there[257] & also to visit his brother who went to America many years ago (in 1872). James died while on this visit, at Toronto, but previously his sister was telegraphed for & she reached there previous to his death. Arrangements having been made, his remains were brought to Barking & [he was] buried in the Churchyard.

1892. King, Joshua (July). Age 53. From Nettlecombe, Somersetshire, he came to Barking, where he was appointed Head Schoolmaster of the National Schools in 1871, & which [post] he held until his death[258]. A few years previously he was compelled to have a leg amputated – since which time his health became affected & eventually [he] died in a fit. His name will always be handed down in connection with the

---

254 Henry Taylor, gentleman, Bull Street. (White's 1848). Henry Vere Taylor was buried on 11th December 1868, aged 23. So William Holmes Frogley would have been 13 years old when he saw the funeral procession.

255 James Pearson, butcher, Trafalgar Place. (Kelly's 1851).

256 John Pearson, butcher, High Street. (Pigot 1833); smack owner, butcher & poulterer, Broadway. (Kelly's 1851). Broadway was known as High Street until late in the 19th century. John Pearson died in December 1858, aged 42.

257 The Chicago World Exhibition was held in 1893.

258 National Schools (boys & girls), Back Lane, Joshua King, master. (Kelly's 1878).

discoveries he made while digging in his garden – the site of a portion of the old Abbey[259].

1888. Wilding, Richard (Oct). He was appointed in 1834 Schoolmaster of the old National School & resigned in 1871 when Mr King succeeded[260]. In later years he was Wharfinger to the Town Quay, and later assisted by his daughters was Registrar of Births & deaths, & Sanitary Inspector (previous to the formation of the Local Board)[261]. During the time Mr Wilding was schoolmaster, his daughter was Mistress of the Girls School[262].

1897. Masters, Charles Thomas – an old inhabitant. Age 82. From 1840 to 1862 he belonged to the Police Force at Barking & retired on a pension. For 20 years later he was a watchman at Trinity Wharf & in 1880 retired from there with a pension.

1883. Bissell, Sarah. Wife of John.

1892. Bissell, John (see North Street)[263]. Jany 1892.

1889. Simmonds, William. April (see Market House)[264].

---

259 Joshua King's excavation of the lady chapel of Barking Abbey took place in 1875-76 (*Essex Times*, 6th May 1876; *Journal of the British Archaeological Association,* 1876, p.112-114). His leg was amputated in University College hospital early in 1886 – he returned to duty in April!

260 Richard Daniel Wilding, master of National School for boys & girls, North Street, and Mrs Anne Wilding, mistress. (Pigot 1839, Kelly's 1851).

261 Richard Daniel Wilding, wharfinger & registrar of births, deaths & marriages, Linton Road. (Kelly's 1878). Richard Wilding was aged 84 when he died. He was one of the enumerators for the 1851 census.

262 Presumably Miss Emily Jane Wilding, formerly at the "high class school", Linton Road. (Kelly's 1878).

263 John Bissell, ironmonger, 6 North Street. (Kelly's 1890). Churchwarden, 1888. *Barking vestry minutes.* 1955. p.318.

264 The family name is, in fact, Simmans, and is frequently misspelt in parish documents and elsewhere. William Simmans (1808-1889) was a gravedigger, later a shoemaker, and also town hall keeper. The vestry minutes record that on 3rd August 1826 William's mother, who was Sexton, was informed that if she continued to employ William about the churchyard, she would lose her position. This was due to his misdemeanours, about which see the next footnote. (Information from Derek Simmans. See also: *Barking vestry minutes.* 1955. p.27).

1891. Simmonds, George. August. Age 51. He was in the building line & all his family was expert bell ringers. He was a son of Simmonds W (1889)[265].

1877. Wade, Joseph. Landlord of the "Barge Aground"[266].

1898. Wade, Elizbeth. Wife of above[267].

1880. Fitt, Edward[268]. Many years a Chemist in the Broadway. (See North Street[269]). Age 69.

1898. Fitt, Ann, Widow of above. Died in her house in the Queens Road. Age 79.

1912. Fitt, Frank, died at Sutton & buried at Barking.

1885. Cutmore, James[270]. He was a twine-spinner in Axe Street & amassed sufficient to retire from business, after building a neat row of houses in the Station Road.

1860. Claringbold, William, succeeded his father – Thomas[271] – as Baker in East Street. The shop was a low wooden structure with tiled roof & the old fashioned round bay window with small square panes of glass.

---

265 George Cabburn Simmans (1840-1891), who was actually aged 52. The name Cabburn commemorates Hannah Cabburn (1814-1881), who was made pregnant at the age of 15 by William Simmans (1808-1889). The child was called William Simmans Cabburn but died, a few weeks old, in 1830. William was forced to marry Hannah, and all their later children were recorded as Simmans. George Simmons (Simmans) was paid £5 for "Organ blowing" in 1865. *Barking vestry minutes.* 1955. p.84. (Information from Derek Simmans and Mark Watson).

266 Joseph Wade, beer retailer, Broadway. (Kelly's 1871). The Barge Aground then stood on the west side of Broadway immediately south of the Market House.

267 Mrs Elizabeth Wade, beer retailer, Broadway. (Kelly's 1878). St Margaret's burial register confirms that she died at the Barge Aground in March 1898, aged 64, although the 1930 register of graves gives 1889.

268 Edward Fitt, chemist & druggist, High Street. (Pigot 1839, White's 1848, Kelly's 1851). Charles Henry Ridley (late Fitt & Son), chemist, 5 Broadway. (Kelly's 1890). Fitt's chemist's shop stood on the east side of Broadway immediately south of Lake & King's corner shop.

269 This section of the manuscript is reproduced in *Mr Frogley's Barking: a first selection.* 2002. p.34-35.

270 James Cutmore, rope & twine maker, Axe Street. (Kelly's 1878).

271 Frogley may have confused the generations regarding the Claringbould family. All available sources between Pigot 1833 and Kelly's 1878 indicate a Thomas Claringbould as the shopkeeper. The rate book of 1829 shows a Richard Belcher as the baker here then,

It stood in its own grounds, surrounded – at the rear & sides – by fine large trees, as I recollect it. At the death of their only son the widow gave up [the] business, & lodged at the house, corner of Church Path, where she died in August 1886. Age 78.

1899. Seabrook, Henry, Senr[272] of the Fishing Smack, Fisher Street. He held the licence about 35 years, & during the time of the Fishery trade had a Blacksmith shop in the rear of the house. (See Fishing smack).

1895. Seabrook, Henry, Son of above, died at Sea.

1910. Seabrook, Elizbeth Charlotte – Widow of above. Oct 1910. Age 76[273].

1895. Carter, Mrs Elizbeth[274]. Widow of Theodore Carter, Grocer &c of Heath Street[275].

It is said that when a young man he was an overseer in the Slave trade, but for upwards of 40 years he resided in Barking. He was succeeded by his son

Alfred[276], but through competition & misfortune was compelled to dispose of the business & eventually was a recipient of the £10 gift[277].

1884. Carter, Theodore. Husband of Above Elizbeth.

---

and the 1851 census suggests that Thomas Claringbold had arrived in Barking between 1829 and 1833. The St Margaret's burial register shows a William Claringbold from East Street was buried on 6th September 1860, aged 99 – perhaps a grandfather who came to Barking at the end of his life.

272 Henry Seabrook, Fishing Smack P.H., Fisher Street. (Kelly's 1890). For the Seabrook family and the Fishing Smack see *Mr Frogley's Barking: a first selection.* 2002. p.54-55.

273 According to Archie Seabrook, grandson of Henry and Elizabeth: " Grandma Seabrook was the ruling factor at the Fishing Smack. Grandpa took a back seat, and apart from fooling about in the cellar, he amused himself chiefly in the blacksmith's shop at the rear of the premises where old Dick Porter (as deaf as a door nail) was in charge. How I used to love to watch old Dick at the anvil, and I was always ready to help operate the bellows at the forge. Grandma was everywhere at once, supervising kitchen duties, the house cleaning, seeing that the customers received their due measure (and no more), and, above all, keeping a very watchful eye on the till".

274 The 1930 register of graves gives Elizabeth's age at death as 89.

275 Theodore Carter, grocer, Heath Street. (White's 1848); Carter & Son, grocers, 25 Heath Street. (Kelly's 1890). Theodore died in 1889, aged 81.

276 Alfred Carter, grocer & provision dealer, Heath Street. (Kelly's 1878).

277 On page 144 of the manuscript, in the section relating to charities, Frogley writes: "Hayes Charity – locally known as the £10 gift. This splendid gift emanated from Mr James Hayes – at one time a resident of Barking. The house in which he resided is not

1891. Garbett, Elizbeth. Age 79. Widow of Miles Garbett who many years previously was lost at sea from a Fishing Vessel. She was a daughter of Mr Jeremiah Holmes of Axe Street [and] mother of James Garbett, Builder of Barking, and Aunt to the Writer[278].

1890. Smith, Mrs, late wife of John Smith, Builder &c of Longbridge Road Barking[279] & formerly landlord of the Anchor & Hope, Barking[280]. He has since married a Jersey lady.

1860. Deveson, Ann, wife of Edward (1890).

1879. Deveson, George, son of above (also 5 more children)[281].

---

positively known, but it was near the Red-Lion in North St. He was described as of Great Surrey St, Blackfriars, London. His wife Elizbeth predeceased him in Nov 1802 & was buried at Little Ilford Church – to the poor of which parish James Hayes was also a Benefactor. By his Will he left the sum of £4000 reduced annuities to be equally divided every year amongst 12 poor parishioners who received £10 each. This charity by his wish was to be transformed by his executors into the hands of the Vicar of Barking for the time being & 3 other persons nominated & appointed by the Vestry of Barking Parish – upon Trust - & apply the Dividends aforesaid in the following manner: "to pay & apply the Dividends of £2000 on the 12th day of February every year, being one moiety of the said £4000, equally to 6 poor house-keepers who do not receive any allowance or support from the said Parish. And upon Trust to apply the second moiety (£2000) as aforesaid on the [ ] day of [ ] every year – no person to partake of the interest of both funds at the same time". As many as 100 people have applied for the gift in one year, and the Trustees consider it a difficult task to decide between the various applicants. Having known a great many who have been the recipients of this Gift I can testify to the fact that no Charity is more impartially & faithfully distributed. It would be very amusing if a Trustee – Mr W. W. Glenny especially – had recorded incidents of the actions &c of those who have received the Gift. How profusely they must have thanked the departed Donor – to whom they can trace no tie or relationship whatever. In February 1891 through the action of Mr Goschen, the then Chancellor of the Exchequer, who reduced the Interest on Government Stock – this once famous [gift] was reduced to £9. The Dividends originally £120 was then only £110. I believe however this only lasted a short time. It may be interesting to know that the original Trustees (1821) appointed was the Vicar the Rev Peter Rashleigh: William Glenny Esq: Charles Welstead Esqr: and Robert Westley Hall Esqr (the latter two from Ilford)".

278 In the 1851 census the 12 year old James Garbett appears in the Axe Street household of William (alias Jeremiah) Holmes, bricklayer, where he is described as a grandson. William Holmes Frogley was also a grandson, since his mother Jane was a daughter of William Holmes.

279 John Smith, builder, Wishford House, Longbridge Road. (Kelly's 1890).

280 The Anchor and Hope pub stood on the West Bank, on the road to Beckton Gas Works.

281 George Deveson died in Newcastle, Natal, South Africa, aged 21, according to the 1930 register.

1890. Deveson, Edward[282] – a Corn & coal merchant in the Broadway and Fisher Street previously Manager of the same business for Mr George Augustus Burrell[283]. A daughter is the wife of Mr Thomas Pelling, Grocer[284], now retired, & a son has also recently retired from a Corn-business previously established by his father[285].

1884. Gosling, Daniel (Oct). He died at his residence Myrtle Cottage, Queens Road. Age 66. His wife survived him many years[286]. For a further account see "The Swan", Queens Road[287].

1881. Moffatt, James, Junior – late Manager for Hewett & Co.

1892. Moffatt, Mrs Mary Ann. See North Street[288].

1881. Moffatt, James[289]. Husband of above Mrs Moffatt.

1892. Cooper, Joseph, Undertaker[290].

Successor to Robert Saggers, Undertaker[291].

---

282 Edward Deveson, corn & coal merchant, oil & cotton cakes, hay & straw depot, Broadway & Fisher Street. (Kelly's 1878). He was a son of John Deveson (1776-1853), farmer of Eastry, Kent, and a younger brother of William Deveson of the Chequers, Barkingside. At 20 years of age he was landlord of the Anchor & Hope, West Bank (1841 census). He was 72 when he died in 1890.

283 George A. Burrell, coal merchant & corn dealer, North Street. (White's 1848). Surveyor, Barking Ward, 1854-67; Churchwarden, 1859-67. *Barking vestry minutes.* 1955. p.318.

284 Agnes, Edward Deveson's youngest daughter, married Thomas Pelling. Thomas Pelling, grocer & agent for W. & A. Gilbey, wine & spirit merchants, 21 Broadway, & grocer & baker, 27 Heath Street & 79 High Street, Plaistow. (Kelly's 1890); Thomas Pelling, 21 East Street. (Kelly's 1895). By 1890 Pelling had branches at Plaistow, Erith, Brentford, Sittingbourne and Maldon.

285 Charles Deveson, corn merchant, 14 Broadway and 118 East Street. (Kelly's 1902). See *Mr Frogley's Barking: a first selection.* 2002. p.39-40.

286 Mrs Gosling, 13 Queens Road. (Kelly's 1890). According to the 1930 register of graves, Mrs Mary June Gosling died in 1892, aged 74.

287 See *Mr Frogley's Barking: a first selection.* 2002. p.149.

288 Mrs Moffatt, Ripple Villa, Longbridge Road. (Kelly's 1890).

289 James Moffat, Hawthorn Terrace, Rippleside. (Kelly's 1871).

290 Joseph Cooper, carpenter, 88 Axe Street. (Kelly's 1890). According to St Margaret's burial register, he was buried on 15th December 1892, aged 78. See *Mr Frogley's Barking: a first selection.* 2002. p. 64 & 73.

291 Robert Saggers/Saggars, carpenter & undertaker, Heath Street. (Pigot 1839, White's 1848, Kelly's 1851).

1900. Quash, Mary, wife of John Quash[292]. See Northbury House.

1902. Quash, John. Husband of Above.

1873. Harwood, Frank (April). Draper adjoining Congregational Chapel[293].

1880. Cooper, Mary[294].

1892. Cooper, James (Husband of Mary above)[295].

1877. Saggers, Robert. Age 84. Undertaker, Heath Street[296].

1873. Hockley, Louisa, wife of Daniel Hockley, Draper of Heath Street[297].

1895. Skinley, Joseph[298]. Age 55. At the age of 16 he was apprenticed to Messrs Hewetts, Fishcarriers &c & remained in their employ until his death. When the Smacks left Barking in 1861 he was sent to Gorleston & became Captain of a Trawler & soon after was appointed Captain of the "Lord Alfred Paget" – a steam carrier that brought the Fish from the North Sea fleet to London. About 1868 he returned to Barking & in 1881, on the death of Mr James Moffatt[299], succeeded him as Manager of Hewetts Works in Fisher Street. He was a staunch Baptist – a member & chairman of the local School Board. He later resided at Southbury House, Hart Street.

1896. Skinley, Sarah Hannah, wife of above Joseph. She died suddenly at 11 Bedford Gardens, Ilford, leaving seven children.

---

292 John Thomas Quash, Northbury House, North Street. (Kelly's 1890).
See *Mr Frogley's Barking: a first selection*. 2002. p.28 & 98.

293 So far as we can discover, the only draper adjoining the congregational Church was Willett's.

294 Mary Ann Cooper died 27th April 1880, aged 64, according to the 1930 register of graves. She was the wife of the Joseph Cooper who died in 1892.

295 James Cooper, undertaker, was the son of Mary Ann and Joseph Cooper, not her husband. He was born on 19th January 1855, married Alice Mills (d. 30th May 1935), and was buried in Rippleside Cemetery.

296 For Saggers family see East of London Family History *Society 1851 census index series: vol.1: part 4*: Essex: Barking. 1984. p.29. See also *Mr Frogley's Barking: a first selection*. 2002. p.64 & 73. Robert Saggers effectively devised his business to his nephew, Joseph Cooper, by his will of December 1874.

297 Daniel Hockley, linen draper, clothier & outfitter, Heath Street. (Kelly's 1871).

298 Joseph Skinley, Southbury House, Hart Street. (Kelly's 1890).

299 Mrs Moffatt, Ripple Villa, Longbridge Road. (Kelly's 1890).

1893. Willett, John. Age 68. Auctioneer, Pawnbroker & Draper[300]. He resided at Braintree House, North Street[301] & his son carried on the business.

1900. Willett, Sophia. Age 74. Wife of above John.

1740. Joyner, John[302].

1748. Joyner, Martha, wife of John.

1826. Milton, Samuel, son of Samuel & Ann Milton, Sailmaker[303].

1857. Milton, John, brother of above Samuel.

1793. Glenny, Ann (of Whitechapel) but of Barking family. Age 55.

1800. Berry, Mary, Mother of above Ann Glenny.

1887. Sivell, David (May). Age 72[304].

1836. Adams, Ann, Mrs (July). Tomb.

1844. Barkly, James. Oct. Age 44. [Page 133]

1893. Barkly, Mary. June. Age 70.

1875. Barkly, William. Dec. Age 51[305]. Husband of Mary & eldest son of James.

1873. Hart, Ann. April. Age 72. Wife of William.

1883. Hart, William. Dec. Age 80.

1862. Bauckham, Robert.

1896. Bauckham, Edwin[306].

---

300 John Willett, draper, Trafalgar Terrace. (Kelly's 1851); pawnbroker, North Street. (Kelly's 1871, 1878). By 1906, Willett's had shops on both sides of the Broadway, East Street and North Street.

301 John Willett, Braintree House, North Street. (Kelly's 1878). John Willett, founder of the business, came from Braintree, where his family were small bankers. (*Barking Advertiser*, 13th January 1923 and information from the late Harold Wand). His son was Robert Willett. See also *Mr Frogley's Barking: a first selection*. 2002. p.40.

302 John Joyner, High Constable 1727-28. *Barking vestry minutes.* 1955. p.322.

303 Samuel Milton, sail maker, Town Quay. (Pigot 1839, White's 1848).

304 David Sivell, shopkeeper, North Street. (Kelly's 1878).

305 Probably William Barkley, butcher, North Street. (White's 1848).

306 Edwin Bauckham, tailor, East Street. (Kelly's 1871).

1860. Milton, Ann, Wife of Samuel Milton, Sailmaker[307]. Mother of two sons mentioned on previous page.

1862. Lynde, Mary. Age 68.

1853. Dawson, Harriett. Sept[308].

1855. Dawson, Elizbeth, wife of Charles. Age 57.

1858. Dawson, Charles, husband of Elizbeth. Age 32.

1860. Dawson, Charles Greenwood. April. Age 65.

1906. Phillips, Elizbeth, da[ughter] of Charles Greenwood. Age 58. Wife of James Phillips.

1860. Butterfield, Ann. Wife of Charles B ----- (Feb)[309].

1833. Forge, John. Sailmaker (June).

1849. Forge, Mary. Wife of John.

1834. Reed, James (son of James & Amelia Reed, relatives to the Forges)[310].

1838. Reed, James. Uncle of Above[311].

1871. Croney, James. Age 64.

1886. Aldous, Richard. Age 49[312]. (See Fisher Street).

1782. Glenny, Alexander. Age 66.

1804. Glenny, Deborah. Age 71 – wife of above.

1883. Shelitoe, Henry. Age 78 (April)[313].

1887. Shelitoe, Mary Ann, wife of above (May), daughter of the following:-

1817. Harris, Joseph, of Mile End. Father of above Mary Ann Shelitoe.

---

307 Samuel Milton, sail maker & smack owner, Town Quay. (White's 1848).

308 According to St Margaret's burial register, Harriett Dawson of Hart Street died on 14th September 1853, aged 1 year 3 months.

309 Charles Butterfield, smack owner. (Kelly's 1851).

310 Died 1834, aged 6 months, according to the 1930 register of graves.

311 Brother, not uncle, "of above" James Reed. Died 1838, aged 8 weeks, according to the 1930 register of graves.

312 Richard Aldous, beer retailer & butcher, Fisher Street. (Kelly's 1878).

313 Henry Shelitoe, smack owner, Heath Street. (Pigot 1839); slopseller & smack owner, Heath Street. (White's 1848); tailor & smack owner, Heath Street. (Kelly's 1851).

1874. Stevens, William C. Clerk at Messrs Lawes, Creekmouth.

1869. Louth, Ellen (Sept). Age 49.

1902. Louth, Joseph, Husband of above. Age 87[314].

1817[?] Hughes, Mary[315].

1830. Hughes, Sarah.

1847. Hughes, John (Husband of Sarah)[316].

Gascoyne Family. [Pages 221-222]

Sir Crispe Gascoyne – youngest son of Benjamin & Ann Gascoyne was born at Chiswick on 1st August 1700. He started the business of a Brewer in Gravel-Lane, Houndsditch, London, and in 1755 his business address was Mincing Lane, when the firm was called "Gascoyne and Weston". In 1741 he was admitted a freeman of the Brewers Company – In 1744 he took the clothing of the Livery – In 1745 [he was] elected assistant – In 1746-7 [he was] elected Master of the Company. In 1745 he was elected Alderman of Vintry Ward – in 1747-8 served as Sheriff and in 1752 was Lord Mayor of London. (Sir Crispe Gascoyne was the first Lord Mayor to reside in the present Mansion House – then recently rebuilt. Also the Lord Mayors Procession was altered this year 1752-3 from 29th of October to 9th November. He is also often quoted in connection with a noted trial heard before him. Two women named Squires and Wells was tried for kidnapping one Elizbeth Canning. His suspicions being aroused he started further enquiries to be made which proved "Cannings" accusations to be false. The mob took the side of Canning – they insulted the Lord Mayor – Sir Crispe Gascoyne – and broke the windows of his stage-coach, and also threatened his life, but upon an enquiry being made, he justified himself to his Liverymen of London who also gave him a vote of thanks). This year – 1752 – he was knighted.

In 1733 he was seated at Byfrons, Barking. This mansion was the property of Dr John Bamber – a wealthy and eminent Physician of Mincing Lane, and

---

314 Joseph Louth, The Bays, Tanner Street. (Kelly's 1890); 23 Tanner Street. (Kelly's 1895).

315 The 1930 register of graves confirms 1817 as the date of death. St Margaret's burial register shows Mary Hughes as aged 13.

316 John Hughes, smack owner, High Street. (Pigot 1839).

who built Byfrons for his country seat. Mr Crispe Gascoyne married his daughter Margaret and so became possessed of the property. Also in 1745 Mr Gascoyne purchased Westbury House. He also purchased other estates in Barking Parish, including the Hospital at Ilford with the right of Presentation and it remains still in his descendants. Sir Crispe died 28 December 1761 and was buried in a Vault in Barking Church, where a handsome monument was erected to his memory. His wife pre-deceased him in 1740. He left four surviving children:- the eldest son succeeded him viz:

Bamber Gascoyne was born in 1725, and after his education at Queens College, Oxford, became a Barrister of Lincolns Inn. At this time he resided at 10 Great Stanhope Street, W. From 1761 to 1786 he was M.P. for Malden: Midhurst: Weabley: Truro and Bossiney. He was Receiver General of Customs and a Lord of the Admiralty. He died in 1791. He was succeeded by his eldest son [Bamber Gascoyne].

(Isaac Gascoyne – 3rd son of Bamber Gascoyne – was born in 1770. He rose from Ensign in the 20th Foot Regiment, and passing through the Coldstream Guards became General of the 54th Foot – later changed to the 1st Dorset Regiment. He died 26th August 1841 at his residence, No 71 South Audley St. London, Aged 72).

Bamber Gascoyne – born 1758 and he was M.P. for Liverpool. He cut off the entail – pulled down Byfrons in 1808 and sold the site and Park. Previous to his death in 1824 he was seated at Childwall Hall, Lancashire. His daughter & heir succeeded him.

Frances Mary Gascoyne. This heiress was married on the 2nd Feburary 1821 to Sir James William Brownlow Cecil K.C., P.C. and Second Marquis of Salisbury – who it is said came possessed – through his Lancashire wife – [of] estates valued at £12000 a year. By Royal Licence obtained previous to marriage, the additional name of Gascoyne was added, and since which time the name of the Salisbury family is "Gascoyne Cecil". Her husband became famous, he carried the Curtana[317] at the Coronation of William IV – [and] was also Lord Privy Seal and President of the Council.

Frances Mary died in October 1839 leaving 3 sons and 2 daughters. Her husband married again to Lady Mary Catherine West, daughter of the Earl of Delaware. The Marquis died in 1868 and his widow afterwards married the Earl of Derby.

---

317 A pointless sword carried at coronations as an emblem of mercy.

The Market-House – or Town-Hall - [Pages 343-346]

is situated in North Street. [It is] an Elizabethan structure mostly of wood and plaster. The lower part originally formed an open arcade, which no doubt constituted the Market and the wooden framework was shewn and the roof was tiled. According to a carved inscription on a tablet annexed to the south wall – outside – the date of its erection was in 1561 or 1567 (the figures are much mutilated)[318]. As stated the weekly market was held in the open portion or arcade. When the Charter was granted I cannot say, but it is said it came from Queen Elizabeth, and according to "Fernside"[319] this sole remaining privilege was transferred in 1836 to Romford Essex. In the Hall above was held the "Court Baron"[320] to decide upon cases of Trespass &c, and also to recover debts under 40/- [321]- but upon the introduction of our modern County Court, it was dissolved. The Royal Coat of Arms was, and I beleive is still to be seen[322].

---

318 Actually 1567. See *Barking and Dagenham buildings past and present.* 1992. p.36. The building was demolished in 1923. (*Becontree Guardian*, 27 July 1923).

319 In the early to mid 19th century, William Gray Fearnside wrote and edited a number of histories of London and the Thames, which Frogley could have consulted in the Guildhall Library. For example, *The history of London*, published in 1838, and *Holmes' Great metropolis, or, Views and history of London in the nineteenth century*, published in 1851. If Frogley is referring to the "privilege" of holding a market, it is highly disputable that it was ever "transferred" to Romford. Under a royal grant of 1247, Romford can object to the establishment of any new market within the judicially accepted radius of 6 and two thirds miles. But Barking's claim would be on the basis of immemorial usage and prescription since references to a market place and tolls there imply the existence of a market back at least to the time of Henry II.

320 By using the term "Court Baron" and not the general term "Manor Court", Frogley wanders into a technical minefield. Up to a point he is quite correct – the sessions of the Manor Court called the Court Baron could deal with cases involving debts or damages of less than forty shillings, and it surrendered this jurisdiction to the County Court under an Act of 1867. However, the main business of the Court Baron was always that of registering the conveyance of copyhold properties, and this continued until 1922, although with decreasing work the General Courts Baron in the Court House were replaced by Special Courts Baron held in various places. There was also another annual session of the Manor Court called the Court Leet that had jurisdiction over many petty offences such as failure to clean ditches or illegal enclosure of roadside waste. It also appointed the local Constables until the Metropolitan Police took over their functions from 1840.

321 Two pounds.

322 The coat of arms has survived and is currently in Court no.1 at the Magistrates Court, Barking.

It will be seen that the date 1837 is shewn also on the wall above the Tablet dated 1561, and I presume by this that the old fabric underwent a thorough renovation, such as the roof slated, [and] the casing timbers around the upper part entirely covered over with plaster. The arcade was closed in and afterwards used as "The Cage" in which was placed disorderly fisher lads and other persons placed for their indiscretions.

In the open space fronting the old building stood the Town-Pump. It was placed there in 1834 and [was] finally removed in 1883. The old "Stocks" also stood here, near the door leading to the Hall above.

The old fabric still stands, although on several occassions those who evidently do not value these old associations have proposed its destruction, but to my knowledge the old place has never lost its usefulness. In 1854, the Provident Bank, instituted for the savings of the poor of the neighbourhood, was held here, having been transferred from the old Workhouse buildings. It had a branch at Ilford, but it was dis-continued in 1887. The lower part – called the Cage – was used for stores, and in 1875 was used by the Lighting Committee as an oilstore for the public lamps. The town was lit up by oil lamps for many years in consequence of a dispute with the Local Gas Company (a full account is given under "Gas Works"). Also the local Fire Brigade was located here after their formation in 1879. There was also a Library[323] attached to it and many other institutions of a useful character. The caretaker had rooms for his residence in the building. His name was William Simmonds, who was also with his sons the local "Bell ringers" at the Church and [a] grave-digger. He died in April 1889 and was buried in a coffin made of material purchased for the purpose of deceased many years previous to his death. The Undertaker was his son "George Simmonds" who also for many years "Blowed" the bellows of the Organ in the Church.

In 1616 this property – of the Crown – was conveyed to Samuel and John Jones, who the same year conveyed it to Thomas Fanshawe (John Jones – This family appears to have resided in this Parish for some generations, and evidently [was] a family of influence. Dr John Bamber of Byfrons also possessed the Manor of Writhfield[324], and at his death in 1753 left Writhfield in trust, to his son in law William Jones Esqr and his wife Charlotte. She died

---

323 Barking Lending Library (Rev. H. F. Seymour, M.A., librarian), Broadway.
324 Should be Wyfield, a manor in Ilford adjacent to Cranbrook.

in 1760 and [was] Buried at Barking, where there is a monument on the North Wall. Probably this William Jones was a descendant). In 1662 Sir Thomas Fanshawe (he was Knighted in ---- [325]) gave in Trust – for the Poor – to the Vicar and Churchwardens the rents of the Market house estate & which comprised [in] later years:- the Market House: the tolls of the Market and Annual Fair, and the adjoining houses – viz the Barge aground beer house and four cottages[326]. He added to this in 1679 the rent of 5 acres of land called "Cotlands". (These five acres was sold in 1895 to the Town Council for £1000 and it now forms part of the Recreation Ground in the Longbridge Road)[327]. These combined form one Charity and was to be distributed as follows:- Three-fifths, together with the sum of £8, to St Margarets, Barking: Two-thirds (less the said £8) to Great Ilford, and out of the portion allotted to Gt Ilford Barkingside was to receive one-fourth. This Estate was let on a lease at a very low rental, and it proved, that after allowing the cost of keeping the fabric in repair and other costs, the poor received next to nothing. The lease expired in 1900, and through the diplomacy of Mr Samuel Glenny[328] this charity I understand is now very remunerative. As great credit

325 Sir Thomas Fanshawe (1628-1705) was knighted in 1660.

326 On page 141 of the manuscript, in the section relating to charities, Frogley writes: "The Market House Estate (this paragraph refers to the Barge Aground Beer-house & 4 adjoining cottages) was let on a Lease which expires in 1900 at a Rental of £20 & the present Lessee had applied to the Overseers to have the Lease cancelled & substitute a new Lease for 40 years at a Rental of £85 per Ann[um]. This offer was made in January 1896 & was accepted by the Overseers – Mr J. W. Parker: A. Burness: G. Mullett & H. R. Steele, but the Commissioners did not then consent, saying they had it under their consideration. Mr Glenny pointed out that had the Overseers succeeded & let this property as desired by the Lessee it would have been a direct loss to the Charity, as he considered there was not only an additional value in the rent, but there was also a premium value. Mr Samuel Glenny estimated the rental value in 1897 to be £130 per ann[um] & the premium value for the Beerhouse to be £2000, and it will be seen that this suggestion of Mr Glenny was practically carried out. A notice dated 16th January 1900 from the Charity Commissioners authorizing the "Estate Trustees" to grant a building Lease of the piece of land together with the Beer-house thereon for a term of 50 years from 25th March 1900 at an annual rent of £75 – the Lessee agreeing to expend not less than £600 in the building & to pay a premium of £200".

327 James Oxley concludes that there were, in fact, two separate pieces of parish land called "Cotlands" or "Cotmans Land". The one mentioned by Frogley was just about in the middle of Barking Park. *Barking vestry minutes.* 1955. p.126 & 315.

328 Samuel Glenny, market gardener, Greatfield, Ripple Road. (Kelly's 1890). For many years he was Chairman of the School Board, Overseer and Poor Law Guardian. Whilst Chairman of the Burial Board, he chose the site of and planned Rippleside cemetery. For

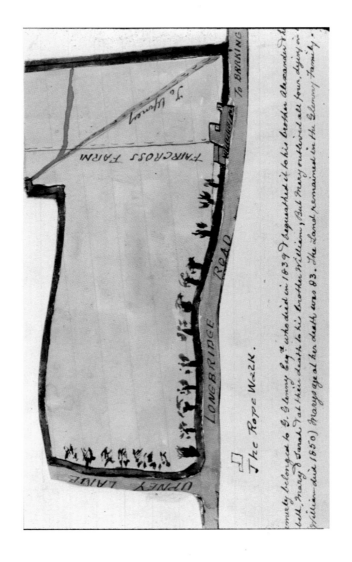

Frogley's plan of the Rope Walk on page 456 of the manuscript. (See page 11).

Stout's watercolour painting of the Rose and Crown in 1904. (See the Milton family on page 88).

Frogley's drawing of the Salvation Army chapel - page 284 in the manuscript.
(See pages 132 - 134).

Portrait of Scrymgeour Hewett (1769 - 1850). (See page 106).

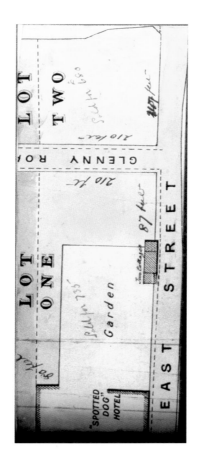

The plan of the Spotted Dog referred to on page 459 of the manuscript. (See page 12).

Frogley's drawing of the Spotted Dog and adjacent cottages in 1890. Page 457 in the manuscript.

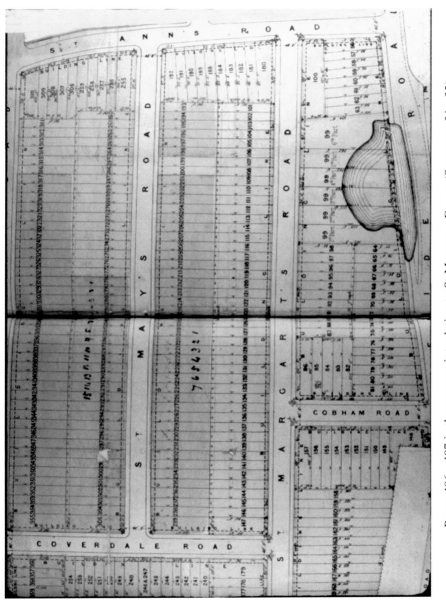

Pages 406 - 407 in the manuscript relating to St Margarets Estate. (See pages 31 - 32). For Frogley's illustration of the pond see page 99.

St Paul's Church, Barking. (See page 30).

is due to Mr S. Glenny I will give a more detailed account of it as given by him at the time.

As stated in the foregoing the lease expired in 1900 at a rent of £20 a year which I presume referred to the Barge aground beer house. The present tenant[329] applied to the Overseers to cancel the Lease and grant a new one for 40 years at a rental of £85 a year. The offer was made in January 1896 and was accepted by the Overseers, viz Messrs J. W. Parker[330]: Burness: Mullett and Mr Steele[331], but the Commissioners did not then acquise[332], saying that they had the matter under consideration. Mr S. Glenny pointed out [that] had the Overseers succeeded, it would have been a direct loss to the Charity. He estimated the rental value in 1897 at £130 and a further premium value for the Beer house of £2000. Accordingly a notice dated 16th January 1900 from the Charity Commissioners, authorising the "Trustees of this Estate" to grant a building lease of the "Peice of land together with the Beer-house thereon, known as the Barge Aground" for a term of 50 years, from 25th March 1900 at an annual rental of £75 – the tenant agreeing to expend not less than £600 in building – and to pay a premium of £2000. I cannot imaging what the said Overseers thought of their lack of judgement, for it is a serious thing for a body of such unqualified men to attempt to administrate upon such matters without seriously seeking the advice and counsel of those who are better

over seventeen years he was Vestry Clerk and Trustee of the Barking General Charities. As a freemason he was a joint founder of two lodges – the Erkenwald Lodge of Barking and the Westcliff Lodge, both of which he was Past Master, whilst also holding high rank in the Loyal Orange Order.

329 Joseph Wade, beer retailer, Broadway. (Kelly's 1871); Mrs Elizabeth Wade, beer retailer, Broadway. (Kelly's 1878); William Foster Wade, beer retailer, Broadway. (Kelly's 1890).

330 On page 264 of the manuscript, Frogley writes: "J. W. Parker [was] born at Brighton in 1863 & came to Barking in 1890 as foreman at the Northern Outfall works, Beckton. He was elected a member of the Town Council & became Vice Chairman. He was also a Member of the Burial Board". Archibald Burness was an "employee at Messrs Hewetts yard as Engineer. He was a progressive & as such entered the Town Council in 1894 & retired 1898. He was one of the unfortunate men killed at Hewetts explosion in Jany 1899". J. G. Mullett was "Another employee of Messrs Hewett & Co as timekeeper & Clerk. He was Secretary to the Progressives party, Member of the Council 1896-7 & at the closing of Hewetts yard he accepted a situation under Mr Marriott, the two of whom was previously great political enemies".

331 On page 274, Frogley writes: "Mr H. R. Steele, Electrical Engineer. As a Progressive was elected a District Councillor 1894-6. He also describes himself as an Evangelist, and has for many years acted as Caretaker of the Quakers Mission Hall".

332 Presumably acquiesce.

informed and competent to pronounce a judgement. By the statement given below it will be clearly seen to what extent the Charity benefitted through the forethought of Mr S. Glenny. In another place is mentioned a suggestion from Mr S. Glenny and which was not supported, but the writer believed that had that suggestion been carried out, it would have been a great boon and blessing to the poor of Barking, and a saving to the ratepayers. (See Workhouse for this suggestion). Mr S. Glenny is an outspoken man and for that reason he was not so popular in Barking as he deserved. I will – in his short biography – mention several matters, some of which have been agreed to and proved well throughout by him, and other matters not supported, but at the same time probably would have been better had they been carried. Anyhow those who read his biography can judge for themselves. The following is the statement referred too:

As per present Arrangements viz 50 years at £75 per Ann[um]	£3750.0.0
An Investment of the Premium, viz £2000 for 50 years at [2.5]%	£2500.0.0
	£6250.0.0
Deduct 10 years – making income for 40 years	£1250.0.0
	£5000.0.0
Adding the Principal on Hand as invested	£2000.0.0
	£7000.0.0
To Contra	
Overseers arrangement – 40 years at £85 a year	£3400.0.0
Balance in hands of Trustees at the end of 40 years	£3600.0.0

And of course additional value in the new buildings[333].

The Church-Path [Pages 66-67]

This very small thoroughfare is a continuation of East Street to the Churchyard. It contains an old wooden fronted house, but as to its original use

---

333 The editor has to admit to completely "losing the plot" on this section. Frogley clearly felt very strongly about this matter, but the finer details of accountancy are not clear, at least to me.

I cannot say definetly. On the front is a half circle with an emblem representing a Bishops Mitre, and by this some have supposed it to have been at one time a vicarage. But I think that it was the residence of Robert Amadas Esqre who held the Manor of Jenkins in 1540[334]. He was a Goldsmith and citizen of London and master of the Kings Jewels. He left Jenkins to reside in a house called "Amadas place" opposite the Abbey Gate[335]. It probably at one time was connected with the Abbey. Of its more modern tenants was a Mr Harris[336] who sold Grocery there; but unfortunately through a fire he lost all his stock &c. He was obliged to move away and shortly after – in 1889 – he was a recipient of the famous £10 gift Charity. A Mr Yellop[337] kept a second-hand furniture shop here until 1898 – the house being divided into two seperate tenements. The house is now (1906) in a wretched condition and is used as a common lodging house, which considering its position in the town & its close proximity to the Church Buildings is a disgrace. There is a rumour that it will shortly be demolished, which would rob Barking of another of its ancient relics. Opposite this house was five cottages, and adjoining them – forming a corner to North Street – was a wooden building or shed used as a Greengrocers. (The shed was kept as a Fruiterers & Greengrocers by Mr Samuel Sutton but after it was pulled down he removed & opened in the same line of business in a shop adjoining the Congregational Chapel[338] & which will be further noticed). This and the Cottages was demolished in 1890 to make room for the large Grocery establishment and warehouses in the rear, erected for Mr Clark. (Mr Clark for many years previously with a partner carried on the business successfully in Heath Street). Before he had sanction to build, the Local authorities [decided] to widen this walk, which was much narrower than now, & for this strip of land the Owners was paid £650. The present Grocers shop & out buildings was erected by Mr Clark at a cost of £1405 and he opened it [on] 26th April 1890, but further additions &

---

334 Robert and Elizabeth Amadas were in possession of Jenkins by 1524. *VCH Essex: vol.5.* 1966. p.199.

335 Amadas Place was actually the house given by Sir Thomas Cambell in his will of 1641 for a Free School in Barking (1663 rental, ERO Sage collection, no.274). The manorial map of 1652/3 shows its position on the east of North Street and south of the Old Vicarage (later Northbury House). Thus it stood opposite the *north* gate of the abbey, and not in Church Path. So Frogley's ingenious conjecture must be discounted.

336 Thomas Harris, grocer, Church Path. (Kelly's 1878).

337 John Yallop, furniture broker, Church Path. (Kelly's 1890).

338 Samuel Sutton, greengrocer & fruiterer, Broadway. (Kelly's 1878).

enlargements was made in 1905. (Mr Argent – Builder & who also kept the "Jolly Fisherman" in North Street – was the builder[339]).

On the other corner is a shop which in 1868 was occupied by Mr Norman, Boot & shoe maker. He left Barking to live at Canning Town & shortly after started as an Auctioneer. He also became a member of the old Local Board of West-Ham and by his efforts the Canning Town portion of Barking Road was paved. Mr W. G. Norman, Auctioneer of Town Hall Chambers, Stratford, is his son.

St Margarets Society of Change Ringers[340]. [Page 84]

This Society was formed in 1870 during the Incumbency of the Rev. H. Jermyn[341], and the following [year] – 1871 – a lamentable accident occurred. A member – Mr Henry Hall, Bailiff to the Lord of the Manor[342] – while ringing his bell, the rope somehow twisted round one of his feet & threw him over with such force, as to injure the spinal chord at the back of his neck & which resulted – 5 hours later – in his death.

In July 1896, four members of the above Society rang a peal of 5058 changes in 2 hours & 27 minutes in the Belfry upon Hand-bells – said to have been the first of its kind in Barking. Also in Nov 1898 the "College Youths" rang upon the Bells of Barking Church a complete peal of Oxford Bob Major of 5058 changes in 3 hours & 7 minutes – said to have been the first peal of Oxford Treble Bob Major rang here since 1761.

The Salvation Army in Barking. [Pages 282-285][343]

There has been a "Corps" of the Salvation Army at Barking for many years,

---

339 David Argent, bricklayer, plasterer, &c, North Street. (Kelly's 1871); Jolly Fisherman & builder, North Street. (Kelly's 1878).

340 Details of the most important peals rung post-1871 are exhibited on the walls of the ringers' loft in St Margaret's Church.

341 Hugh Willoughby Jermyn, MA, Vicar. (Kelly's 1871).

342 Kelly's 1871 lists Henry Hall, Ches(t)nut Villa, Queen's Road (private resident) and Henry Hall, basket maker, Fisher Street. For a full account of this accident, see *Essex Times*, 11th November 1871.

343 Frogley covers nonconformity in Barking on pages 277-300. His detail of recent events probably came from newspaper accounts and personal knowledge, but he has gone to some length to document the history of all religious sects in the town.

and the opposition they experienced at one time caused a great many converts to discontinue the Army. They originally met for their meetings in a room over a house opposite the Town Quay, and which I beleive was used as a sail loft during the time the Fishing smacks came to Barking. They called it the "Bethel" and lively times they had from the opposition. They had good supplies of officers from headquarters, and one officier at this time was sent down specially to move the members of the Barking contingent "up a bit". On one Sunday morning in 1881 there was a great muster here with their lady Captain[344], assisted by specially imported officers "to make a special attack upon his Satanic Majesty". The party had concertinas, tambourines, triangles and of course the big drum and the afternoon especially proved a very exciting time. On the Tuesday following a brass band was sent down from Headquarters, and the Army members went through what they termed their "War Dances" to the amusement of those looking on. In January 1883 Captain Garry – a local officer – promised the people of Barking that in the future, on Sundays, he would stir them up. A report in the War Cry at that time said of Barking: "We had our brass band out for the first time. The town was all up in arms, the Devil raging and Saints rejoicing. At our Consecration making the power of god came down – The testimonies at the free and easy were good &c". Also at this time the Captain and his sub-officers wore red guernseys[345] for the first time. The army made good progress and in 1891 purchased the small chapel in Ripple Road, and of which I will now give its short history.

In the article upon the "Baptists" the Rev G. J. Gillinghams name was mentioned as Pastor, but through some dispute he with a few members resigned and later hired the Temperance Hall for preaching in. After three months, finding his followers increasing, a peice of land was purchased on the Westbury Estate, Ripple Road and an iron building erected at a total cost of £600. Of this amount £250 was advanced by the Baptist Building Fund for

---

344 *VCH Essex: vol.5*, p.245 is even more emphatic than Frogley that "Barking was one of the earliest centres of Salvation Army work". Station 15 of Booth's Christian Mission (the predecessor of the Salvation Army) was opened in 1873 at the "Old Bethel" in Barking, which had been in existence before 1870 (*Essex Times*, 31 September 1870). Miss Anne Davis, their "lady Captain", mentioned by Frogley, arrived in 1875, before the name Salvation Army was adopted in 1878.

345 A thick knitted, woollen outer tunic or jersey.

10 years free of Interest, and a greater portion of the other £350 was raised by Concerts, Bazaars, Collections &c. It was opened on 26th April 1887 by the Revd C. Spurgeon[346]. During the first year the Pastor and members worked hard to increase their numbers – holding 483 meetings during that year. In March 1888 a sale of work was held in the Chapel in order to reduce the existing debt of £320, and at the same time it was proposed to effect a scheme, by issuing £250 in £1 shares, so that – with collections – the whole debt could be wiped out in two years. The Bazaar mentioned appeared tolerably successful. In the centre of the Chapel was erected a representation of a huge ship laden with articles of the most useful character. A Sunday School being formed was well attended, and the British & Foreign Bible Society presented the Bibles and Testaments to the value of six-guineas. There was two excursions to High-Beach, the first in August 1887 and the other on 2nd July 1888, but after three years struggle, the Rev G. J. Gillingham preached his farewell sermon on Sunday 29th Sept 1889, the service being represented by the presence of members from the other denominations of the town – including the Parish Church and the Salvation Army. The Pastor, referring to the up-hill struggle experienced to make the Chapel self-supporting, had undermined both his and his wifes health.

In January 1890 the Trustees of the Chapel met to consider a request from the newly formed Barking School Board, who was desirous of hiring the Chapel for a temporary day school, but the Trustees unamiously resolved "not to let the building for school purposes but were willing to sell the property". This the Board declined to do, but it was eventually sold to "General Booth" of the Salvation Army, and it was opened on the 14th Feburary 1891 by Major Stiff from the Property department London. Previous to the opening the "Army" had the platform taken down and a new one erected with tiers of seats for the members.

Congregationals. [Pages 286-288]

This body is the oldest sect of the Dissenters in Barking. They appear to have originated here in consequence of the Rev Edward Keighley[347] – a minister

---

346 Charles Haddon Spurgeon (1834-1892) was England's best-known preacher for most of the second half of the nineteenth century.

347 Edward Keighley's name was most commonly written and pronounced Keightley. His father, also Edward, married Isabel, widow of Thomas Barnes (d.1626), owner of

of the Church of England, being silenced at the Restoration. His family owned Albro Hatch and he was Chaplain to the Chapel attached to the Mansion, after his ejection from the Church. In July 1672-3 he obtained a Licence for a house at Barking for preaching, and this body became "Independents" or Congregationalists. Dying in June 1701 he was buried at Barking. He was succeeded by the Rev Richard Taylor, who was also one of the ejected ministers[348]. He came from Holt, county of Denbigh. He appears however to have acted as "Clerk" during the Vicarship of the Rev Thomas Cartwright at Barking Church. He joined this body and dying in 1697 was buried near the pulpit in Barking Church. For several years after his death, nothing is recorded of this body, and no doubt they became extinct. In 1782, the Revd George Gold, a Congregational minister of Stratford[349], hired a house at Barking and preached there, thus reviving the defunct congregation, and in 1784 the first chapel was erected[350], but this was soon enlarged. In 1804 the Rev J. K. Parker of Upminster preached here, and by request, he accepted the Pastorship in Sept 1804. The next year the Chapel was enlarged at a cost of about £60. He died in 1817 and during his 13 years pastorship 50 members were added. The next elected minister was the Rev J. West in November 1819 and [he] continued here for 16 years, adding 27 new

Aldborough Hatch. It is probable that the son, after graduating at Oxford in 1654, became the first and only minister of the "new chapel" at Barkingside. Expelled from there at the Restoration, he continued to minister at a chapel attached to his mother's house at Aldborough Hatch, where he was licensed as a Presbyterian preacher in May 1672. *VCH Essex: vol.5*, p.230-231.

348 There is no evidence to support Frogley's suggestion on page 95 of the manuscript that Richard Taylor was a "curate under Dr Cartwright". Legally he was an expelled "dissenter", probably held a "conventicle" at his own house, and advocated Presbyterianism. However, he was Cartwright's tithe collector and apparently regarded himself to his death still as an ordained minister – *a clerk in holy orders* – of a Church of England which might again become comprehensive. Moreover, he was the well-to-do tenant of Westbury, a regular attender at the Vestry from 1670, and held various parish offices. (Bert Lockwood discusses this anomalous position in his forthcoming *Tithe and other records of Essex and Barking*).

349 "In 1782 George Gold, minister of the Brickfields Congregational church in West Ham, began to hold services in a hired house at Barking". *VCH Essex: Vol.5*. p.231.

350 The Congregational Chapel stood on the east side of Broadway directly opposite the Market House/Town Hall. See the map of Broadway illustrated in *Mr Frogley's Barking: a first selection*. 2002. p.139.

members[351]. He resigned in 1835 to another Chapel at Bethnal Green. The Revd J. Corney succeeded in 1836[352]. (Mr Corney came from Wycliffe Chapel, Mile End – then under the Pastorship of the Rev Dr Andrew Read, who also occcassionaly preached at Barking. The Anniversary was – as now – held yearly, but in those days it was held in the old Town-Hall, when a substantial tea was provided. Annually the members of Wycliffe Chapel came down to Barking in conveyances from Mile-End. Mr Corney after leaving Barking went to live at Stockport, and he died there in April 1862. His son in law – Mr Lea – and who also had preached here, died suddenly at Stratford main railway station in 1893 and Mr Corneys eldest son was living at East-Ham in 1895. During Mr Corneys pastorship at Barking he resided at Vine Cottage, Tanner Street and also at Roden Lodge. He conducted the burial service over Mrs Elizabeth Fry).

In 1842 a meeting was held for the purpose of starting a fund for building a new church and in 1846 a Tea-meeting was held at the Town Hall when a statement was made that the church was built and paid for. It cost £560. There was no music at this time in the chapel – the singing being led by a Mr Belcham[353]. In 1851 this church was repaired, and it was decided to build a schoolroom at the rear, upon land purchased in 1850. Mr Corney resigned in 1860 in consequence of bad-health and was succeeded by the Revd J. Smedmore[354]. The foundation stone of the present building – as shewn in the above view – was laid in 1863 by Isaac Berry Esqr of Chelmsford and the new Church was opened in 1864. It cost £2100. Mr Smedmore also founded the day-school, the foundation stone of which was laid by Mr John Curwen of Plaistow, and it was formally opened by Mr Vaizey, High Sheriff of Essex. The School and classrooms cost £1300. Mr Smedmore resigned – adding few new members – and was succeeded by the Rev J. H. Stanley who did not remain long, and in 1883 was succeeded by the Rev T. Davies[355]. In 1884 the Chapel underwent thorough renovation. The Harmonium that stood in the

351 In 1829 the congregation was estimated at 350-400. (Essex Record Office, Q/CR 3/2).

352 Rev. George Corney, Independent Minister. (White's 1848); Independent Chapel, High Street, Rev G. Corny, minister. (Kelly's 1851).

353 Isaac Belcham, baker, Fisher Street. (White's 1848); baker & grocer, Fisher Street. (Kelly's 1871).

354 Congregational Chapel, Broadway, Rev Joseph Smedmore, minister. (Kelly's 1878).

355 Congregational, Broadway, Rev. Thomas Davies, minister; 11am & 6.30pm; Wed 7.30pm. (Kelly's 1890); Rev.Thomas Davies (Congregational), 23 Linton road. (Kelly's 1895).

Gallery was replaced by a pipe organ at the East end, at a cost of £225. During the alterations the Chapel was closed for three weeks. The Platform was brought further into Chapel, and the whole building was better lighted. Hot water pipes were introduced in the place of two iron stoves for heating the chapel, and the ceiling decorated, at a total cost of £500.

In 1888 a Bazaar was held in the schoolroom (on the 8th & 9th of March) in aid of the Church funds, & was opened by Mr Rumsey of Stoke-Newington. In 1891 the membership was 101, being an increase of 38 since 1883. In 1892 another Bazaar was held, to remove the debt incurred in replacing the windows of the Church and Vestry at a cost of about £90.

The Rev J. Davies the present Pastor (1898) has promoted several charitable schemes. In 1886 through his endeavours a fund was raised to relieve those thrown out of employment by the closing of the Jute Works. Several were sent to Canada and otherwise assisted. The amount spent out of this Fund up to 1893 exceeded £1000. In January 1894 the "Home Messenger", a monthly magazine, was first issued by this body – also in July of the same year the Burial ground was closed for Burials by an Order from the Home Office[356]. In this burial ground lies the remains of several old inhabitants and members of this body, among whom are several members of the Earle family – smackowners of the town[357]. Also Mr William Grainger[358] Grocer, died May 1892. Mrs Mary Earle died 1883[359]. She was the wife of Henry Earle, mast and block maker and later landlord of the "Still" Fisher Street. He died at Grimsby.

Brethren[360]. [Page 291]

There are two sections of this body in Barking – one is known as the "Exclusive Brethren" who admit only those who are in Fellowship with them

356 The human remains were removed from the burial ground to Rippleside Cemetery in November 1928. The Chapel was finally closed in 1929 and the building converted into a covered market. (Information from Miss Gwen Cooper).

357 Henry and John Earle, smack owners. (White's 1848, Kelly's 1851).

358 William Grainger, grocer, Broadway. (Kelly's 1878)

359 Mrs Mary Earle was a sister of Joseph Frogley, and therefore the aunt of William Holmes Frogley, the author. It was Joseph who arranged for the widow's body to be brought from Camden Town to Barking for burial in 1883. He was an executor to her will and a principal legatee.

360 More widely known as Plymouth Brethren.

to take the Sacrament, and the "Open Brethren" whose "table" is open to all members of any sect. Both sections have been in Barking many years, and the principle supporters was the "Glenny" family.

The Exclusive Brethren meet for worship in the upper part – now Messrs Page Calnans showroom, at the corner of Fisher Street. Under this large room was at that time a large store or coal shed, and Mr Benjamin Glenny was the owner, a builders merchant and contractor. They were an earnest body, but disputes among them continuously arose, and eventually the majority left the above building and met at the house (residence) of Mr Glenny in East Street until he left the town and the house was pulled down. In 1901 they converted a large stable or store into a meeting place and are there now (1898). This is situated in the Linton Road, and was the property of W. W. Glenny Esqr, who was also one of their members.

The Open Brethren met in a small chapel in Axe Street, and another section of the Glenny family was chief here, viz Mr Edward Glenny of Byfrons. In the rear of this chapel is a small burial ground, and where several members of both sections were buried. Edward Glenny son of Mr Glenny of Byfrons was always an energetic preacher. The members of this body increased more so that[361] the other section and in 1884 they built a new hall in Axe Street. It is called "Park Hall" and seats some 600 people. The old building they retained as a Sunday School. Edward Glenny is still an energetic member of this body and is the head of the North African Mission[362]. Several times I beleive he has travelled on behalf of this Mission whose local head-quarters is in the Linton Road.

Catholics. [Page 292]

This important body for many years was practically the only religion of this country, therefore previous to the dissolution of Religeous Houses in the 16th century, the whole of the population of Barking was Roman Catholics, and no doubt the then existing generation continued in the religeon, although the law of the country prohibited the preaching or practice of it. During Marys reign things were again altered in their favour, and it was again preached in

---

361 Than.

362 North Africa Mission Office (Edward H. Glenny, Hon.Sec), 19 & 21 Linton Road. (Kelly's 1890).

the Church. After her death in 1558 the law was so rigorous that I doubt if any attempt was made to revive it, until about the year 1857, when Father Benfield commenced to preach in the open air at Barking. Mr Benfield was formerly a clergyman of the Church of England and therefore a convert to the Romish faith. It is said he was much troubled with the modern interpretation of the Bible, and subsequently beleived that the Church of Rome only could interpret it. Preaching at Barking in the open air a few times and meeting with several Catholics at Barking and Wall-end – and he being a wealthy man – had erected in 1857 a small building at the rear of he present church in Linton Road. It contained an Alter and the necessary vestments for the Service of Mass in the morning and a Benediction for evening. The Rev Father Benfield is now dead, but in 1897 he was priest and Superintendent of the Roman Catholic Schools, Barnet. He was succeeded by the Revd Father Gillingham (he was not a convert)[363]. After preaching in the old chapel for many years, the present handsome church was erected in ---- [364] and dedicated to "SS Mary and Ethelburga" – the opening ceremony was conducted by the late Cardinal Manning. Later (in ----) the Presbytery and Boundary wall was built at a cost of £750. Father Gillingham died in 1887 and [was] buried at Ilford Cemetery and the Rev D. Hickey was appointed Priest[365]. He – as was the case with his predecessor – is very popular, and highly respected by all classes and creeds in the town. In 1889 the "old church", which had been used for school purposes, was demolished, and the present commodious Schools erected on its site. They were opened in September 1889 to accommodate 220 Children. At the opening ceremony an excellent tea was given to the children by Mrs Cox – their late mistress. This lady is also Organist of the Church. In December 1895 the Rev Father Hickey resigned and was presented by the congregation with a "Chalice" as bearing testimony to the zeal with which he laboured in Barking. He was succeeded by the Rev A. W. Clements, the present Priest.

---

363 According to *VCH Essex: vol.5*, p.245, the first priest was Edward Lescher. He was succeeded by James Gilligan in about 1860. Catholic Church, Linton Road, Rev James Gilligan, priest. (Kelly's 1871, 1878). Frogley confuses this Roman Catholic priest with the Baptist minister, Revd. Gillingham.

364 1869. *VCH Essex: vol.5*, p.245.

365 SS Mary & Ethelburga Catholic, Linton Road, Rev. David Hickey, priest. (Kelly's 1890, 1895).

Friends. [Page 295]

The Society of "Friends", or Quakers, was settled in Barking or its neighbourhood at a very early period of their foundation as a society[366]. On the 2nd August 1664, Thomas Salthouse and four other Quakers was fined £5 for being at a meeting house at East-Ham, and for non-payment was committed to Barking prison for two months ([Reeves hist of Quakers][367]). Their history at Barking partly – as follows - is from a local source and I beleive authentic. In 1673 a part of an old Mansion – known as Taits Place – was purchased from William Mead for £87, in consequence of its delapidated condition. This William Mead was a large landowner in Barking, and being son-in-law to George Fox, the founder of this Society[368], no doubt accounds[369] for their early introduction into Barking. This remains of a large mansion, and purchased as stated, was an oak-timber building of the Tudor period, and was built about 1500. This was used as a meeting house by the "Friends" and in one room – still preserved – is some oak panelling and which the Trustees a few years ago refused £600 for. In 1758 it was not rebuilt as stated by some, but much altered and modernised, and the front was bricked[370]. The cause of this outlay was because the place had a narrow escape of destruction through a severe storm, but the Oak Parlour and a portion of the carcase[371] was saved[372]. The cost of this renovation was £233.

---

366 Quakers at Barking are mentioned as early as 1658. (Terry Philpot, "Barking Friends", *Barking Record*: no.87, 1974, p.5). They probably met at a former Meeting House in Fisher Street indicated as such in the Manorial Survey (ERO D/DHs M31, fo.27).

367 Thomas Henry Reeves: *The planting of Quakerism in England.* 1896.

368 William Mead (1628-1713) was owner of Gooshays in Havering and a friend of George Fox, according to *VCH Essex: vol.5*, p.232. His wife, Sarah, was a step-daughter of George Fox. The only ornate tombstone in the Barking burial ground marked William's grave of 1713.

369 Accounts.

370 Frogley's illustration in the manuscript shows the front of the old Quaker Meeting House at some date prior to 1905. It may be compared usefully to Bamford's water-colour drawing of 1905 which is illustrated in *VCH Essex: vol.5* and elsewhere and which shows a similar front-view but with a small extension to the left. Both illustrations support the view that the house was refronted in 1758, not entirely rebuilt.

371 Alternative spelling of carcass.

372 This "severe storm" damage was reported to the Monthly Meeting on 3rd March 1705 ("The early records of the Monthly Meeting of the Society of Friends", *Transactions of Barking Historical Society*, 1960, p.7).

In front of the Oak Parlour was a larger room with a platform, and as one entered this apartment and stood before this platform, how reverently would that one think of Elizabeth Fry, whose voice, her small congregation heard there so many times.

Very little progress appears to have been made in Barking by this Society, and the Meeting House was continually closing or [was] let for other purposes, but they evidently retained a portion for funeral and other special meetings. Mrs Elizabeth Fry on one of these occassions attended a meeting here in 1816. In 1809 it was used as a Brew-house, and attached to it was a coach house and stables, belonging [to] Mr George Spurrell[373]. They ceased to hold their meetings here in 1830. (Mr Samuel Gurney on 7th April 1838 was married to Elizabeth Shepfherd at this Meeting House[374]). About 20 years later and for many years, Mr Henry Ault, of Church Road, Barking[375], had a private school here. (Singularly, Richard Claridge – mentioned [below] - kept a boarding school here from 1700 to 1706, but he was a Quaker, and Mr Ault was a Church of England attendant). The "Friends" under more modern forms opened the hall again for mission work, and in 1895 [an] additional hall of corrugated iron was erected adjoining the old building – to seat 250 persons. All these buildings were demolished in 1901 and a larger building erected on its site. As stated the valuable oak panelling is preserved in the original parlour – a room 16 feet x 14 feet. With a small exception this room is lined from floor to ceiling with this panelling.

The new building, called the Assembly Hall, was opened on 20th May 1908. The "Hall" is 55 feet long, 30 feet wide and 25 feet high. Adjoining is a room 30 feet x 20 feet which contains a platform and the Oak-panelling. There is also two classrooms – one of which is the famous oak-parlour. The old

---

373 George Spurrell, Surveyor 1751, Churchwarden 1758-9, Overseer 1763, 1780. *Barking vestry minutes.* 1955. p.325.

374 Samuel Gurney, Elizabeth Fry's brother, married Elizabeth Sheppard, daughter of James Sheppard of Ham House, at the Barking Meeting House in April 1808, not 1838. Janet Whitney: *Elizabeth Fry.* 1937. p.116.

375 Henry Ault, gents' boarding school, North Street. (Kelly's 1851). The 1851 census shows Henry Ault conducting a boarding school at Roding Lodge with 16 resident scholars, mainly London born, between 6 and 14 years of age. Perhaps he used rooms in the Meeting House across the road as well. He is not listed in Kelly's 1855, but in 1875 Henry Ault, schoolmaster, aged 84, was one of the 12 deserving poor receiving £10 from the Hayes Charity (*Essex Times*, 13th February 1875).

building was enclosed by a heavy looking brick wall, but the present frontage to Queens Road and North Street is enclosed by plain wrought iron fencing. The entrance porch contains some bricks from the old building with the name of Richard Claridge on them – supposed to have been cut in by himself. On the opposite side of the road is a peice of land enclosed by an old wall[376]. It is their "Burial Ground"[377]. Originally it was part of an orchard but in 1672 the "Friends" purchased it – about half an acre – for this purpose. The ground was the property of Mr Edward Burling. There were several members of the Quakers buried in the Churchyard. In 1662 "Ewers" a Quaker & in 1663 a John Ruddell, Quaker, from the Burial Register. In the Burial Ground was buried Mr Samuel Gurney in 1856 and 88 carriages attended his funeral. Joseph Fry and Elizabeth Fry, with some of their children, was also buried here[378].

Mrs Elizabeth Fry. [Page 297]

This estimable lady, was a daughter of Mr John Gurney, who claimed descent from an Ancient Norman family. By the 18th century the "Gurneys" was engaged in commerce – John Gurney, father of the above Elizabeth, was a wool stapler, and later became a partner in the Norwich Bank. His wife – Catherine Bell - was the grand daughter of the famous Robert Barclay of Ury. In 1786 Mr & Mrs Gurney removed to Earlham, near Norwich, and both families were prominent members of the "Friends". They had 12 children, and of whom Elizabeth with her sisters attended a lecture given by "Friend" named Savery, and from that day Elizabeth adopted the doctrine and dress of the "Friends". On 12th August 1800 she married Mr Joseph Fry, who was a partner in his fathers house of Business at St Mildreds Court, London, and where they at first resided.

---

376 In February 1702, "it was decided to build a brick wall 6 feet high before the burial ground with a pair of gates". *Transactions of Barking Historical Society*, 1960, p.7.

377 The Quaker burial ground was vandalised in 1979. The *Observer* (28 October 1979) reported the outrage with the phrase "desecrated by vandals last week" when "the half-acre plot was being tidied up by young people on a Government job creation scheme". The following year the Society of Friends leased the ground to Barking & Dagenham Council who removed the remains of the stones and turned it into an open space with a memorial.

378 Mrs Elizabeth Fry, East Ham; John Gurney Fry, Little Ilford; Joseph Fry, junior, East Ham; William Storrs Fry, East Ham. (Pigot 1839, Barking section, Gentry).

Mr Fry Senr dying in 1808, [Page 298]

they removed from London to Plashet House, East-Ham. Here they experienced both joy & sorrow & shortly afterwards they lost their daughter – 4 years old - Elizabeth, who was buried at Barking. In 1828 the failure occurred of the business in which Mr Fry was partner, which forced them to leave Plashet House to reside with their son at St Mildreds Court, London; but subsequently they removed back to Plashet House for a short time, then removing to the "Cedars" West Ham Park, the property of her brother Mr Samuel Gurney. She died at Ramsgate 12th October 1845 and was buried in the "Friends" burial ground at Barking. Close by was buried her daughter Elizabeth: Samuel Gurney her brother: Elizabeth Fry her sister in law and many other members of the united families. How often does anyone when passing this apparently insignificant spot, pause, to think there is laying there the mortal remains of one of the greatest of women philthramphists[379] that ever lived. The only memorial to her is a plain head-stone on the North side of the Burial Ground bearing the following inscription:

Joseph Fry

died 1861

Aged 84

Elizabeth, wife of

Joseph Fry

died 1845

Aged 65

---

379 Philanthropists.

In the article upon "Dagenham Gulf" is a further account of how this good Lady usually resorted to that spot annually with her family in the same manner as the "Seaside" is resorted in these days.

Methodists[380]. [Page 289]

This body preached at Barking first about the middle of the 19th century and their present chapel was built in 1856. It is situated in the Manor Road[381]. In 1868 by hold[ing] tea-meetings, Barzaars &c money was raised sufficiently to lengthen the chapel at the rear and the whole redecorated. In 1883 the[y] received £50 from a fund given to the cause by James Duncan Esqr, with which they at Barking purchased a peice of land in the Longbridge Road nearly opposite the Spotted Dog, but they never made any use of it. I have very little to record of this body – their minister was supplied from the Circuit as is usual with that sect. Thirty years ago, and for some years after, they appeared to be progressing and certainly increasing in membership, and by purchasing the land in Longbridge Road it was evident that they anticipated erecting a larger building where a new and populous district was certain to come in the course of a few years. For some reason their project was abandoned and the land sold. It was later acquired by the Railway Company for their recent improvements.

Wesleyans. [Page 300]

According to one source the Wesleyans made their appearance in Barking about 1785 – probably this refers to Mr Wesleys Journal which says that he preached at Barking on 6th January 1784, and in the evening at Purfleet[382]. Mr Lysons also mentions them, but there is no evidence that as a body they existed in the town until many years after. Previous to 1830 there was only one dissenting body here – the Congregationals. It would be this time, or a

---

380 Frogley's treatment of Methodism is unsatisfactory in several respects. Wesleyan Methodism, in the broad sense of the Conference and Connexion, must be regarded as mainstream Methodism (even if it was the habit in Frogley's Barking to refer to its adherents simply as "Wesleyans"). Primitive Methodism was a breakaway body, established nationally in 1811, and notwithstanding evangelical activity remained a minority sect. Since the Wesleyan section in the manuscript has no heading of its own, it may be that Frogley intended to reposition it himself in front of that on Primitive Methodism.

381 Primitive Methodist Chapel, Manor Road, ministers various. (Kelly's 1878).

382 John Wesley visited Barking in 1783 and 1784. *VCH Essex: vol.5*, p.233.

Page 281 in the manuscript. (See page 156).

Charabanc outing from the Thatched House pub. (See pages 38 -39).

THE TOWN HALL. 1890.

Page 344 in the manuscript. (See pages 118 - 120).

147

Extract from the memoirs of Thomas Tyser relating to the building of Ripple Castle. He had already built two houses at Rippleside called "Leisure Hour Cottages". (See page 39)

Upney Lane, Barking

See page 52 for Frogley's description of rural Upney Lane.

Samuel Glenny (d.1910). (See footnote 328 and *Mr Frogley's Barking*, p.135-136).

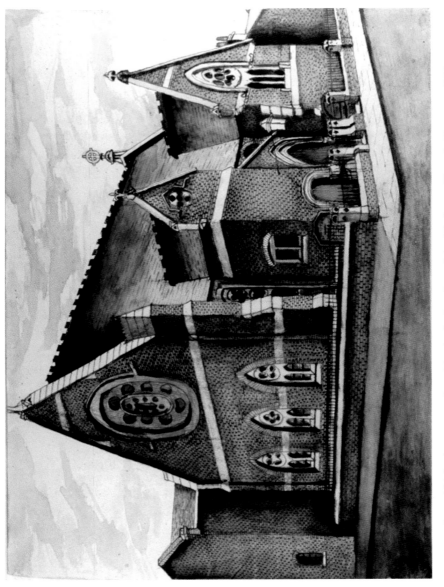

Page 299 in the manuscript - Frogley's drawing of the Wesleyan Chapel. (See page 153).

Westbury House in 1871. (See page 34).

little later, that the[y] had a meeting house in the town and soon built a chapel in East Street[383]. This was demolished in 1869 and the present building erected on its site. The foundation stone was laid by Sir Francis Lycett – a gentleman who gave £1000 each towards the building of Wesleyan Chapels provided they was built in a certain time, and he limited the number to 40. Of this offer Barking took advantage. It seated 600. In 1888 thieves entered the Chapel at night but there was nothing to take, except some books. In 1889 the chapel was re-decorated, & warming appliances added at a Cost of £130. In Feburary 1891 a Bazaar held for three days to clear this debt off was well attended, and in June 1892 another was held to defray the cost of enlargening the Vestry which cost another £70. In 1894 the Local Authorities purchased the boundary wall at the side of the Chapel. This wall was the only portion left remaining of the old chapel demolished in 1869. The Schools in the Rear seats about 400 children – and this number attended the day school. They were erected in 1894, but in 1897 the attendance became so small that it was decided to close them. They were opened again in January 1898 when 130 Scholars was on the books. The Master – Mr Pink[384] – in March 1898 was appointed Registrar of Births & Deaths on the death of Mr Richard Wilding[385]. In 1884 the church members numbered 140 and in1898 there was 180 members.

Baptists[386]. [Pages 277-282]

This body appears to have originated in Barking early in the 19th century. The Baptist churches of Essex united in 1812 for the purposes of villiage preaching and their first Anniversary was held the same year of Raleigh,

---

383 The first Wesleyan chapel in Barking, a wooden building at the western end of East Street, was licensed in 1797 but was in use before that. *VCH Essex: vol.5*, p.233.

384 (1) William Pink, deputy registrar of births, deaths & marriages, Barking town sub-district, Romford union, Wesley house, Longbridge road. (2) Wesleyan school (mixed), East Street, for 356 children; average attendance, 344; William Pink, master. (Kelly's 1890). Pink is listed as master in 1878.

385 Richard Daniel Wilding, registrar of births, deaths & marriages, North Street. (Kelly's 1871); wharfinger & registrar of births, deaths & marriages, Linton Road. (Kelly's 1878).

386 The early history of the Baptists in Barking, and particularly Ilford, is better covered in *VCH Essex: vol.5*, p.232-233, but Frogley's coverage of their later history in Barking is fuller than that in *VCH Essex: vol.5*, p.243.

Essex[387]. (In 1814 there was Baptist Chapels at Ilford, Thaxted, Loughton, Walthamstow and other Essex towns and villages). Several old inhabitants informed me of some of this sect holding open air preaching, near the pond in front of the Abbey Wall, and as is their tenets, while they preached "immersion" the people frequently immersed them in the pond. The earliest record I have of them as established here was in the year 1846, when the[y] obtained licence from the Bishop of London to preach in a house, on the site of the present Duke of York public house[388]. So little progress did they make that in 1850 there was only six members, but these formed themselves into a church and at once took steps to secure a more convenient place for their meetings. A site was purchased in the Queens Road for £45 and a building costing about £200 was erected upon it and including legal expenses the total cost was £280. In July 1851 the chapel was opened and for some time the ministry was by supplies. In 1855 Mr J. Dawson was ordained as their first pastor, and who resigned in 1860. In 1861 The Rev David Taylor (also a Dyer & Cleaner of Mile End) became Pastor. He was a man of short stature, and being a sincere and zealous man in the cause, the congregation & members greatly increased. During his time he preached from a pulpit, but this was taken down and a platform erected. The Sunday School also filled the chapel, so it was decided either to enlargen the chapel, or build another. Plans were submitted to extend the front of the foot-path, but this was abandoned. At this time a leading member was a blind-man named "Hall". He was a very successful basket maker in Fisher Street[389], but later built larger premises in East Street – now demolished.

The Rev David Taylor resigned in 1873 and later accepted the ministry of the Baptist Chapel at Chadwell Heath and is there now (1898). The Rev J. Tompkins succeeded[390]. He was a student from the Metropolitan Tabernacle. The first day he preached, he said, there was only about 48 persons present

---

387 Rayleigh.

388 The site of the Duke of York in East Street was once the Cock beer house. Further evidence for this being where the Baptists met is provided in the obituary of Joseph Jackson (c.1805-1885), the father of Barking's first librarian George Jackson: "The Baptist Church was first formed in a little room where the Cock beer house in East-street now stands, and this had Mr Jackson for one of its founders. Deceased was also for many years one of the deacons of the chapel after its removal to Queens-road" (*Essex Times*, 10th January 1885).

389 Henry Hall, basket maker, Fisher Street. (Kelly's 1871).

390 Baptist Chapel, Queens Road, Rev. J. Tomkins, minister. (Kelly's 1878).

at two services. He was offered a salary of £70 a year, but as he thought he should probably get married, he considered it was not enough, accordingly it was increased to £78 a year, and a year later was increased to £100. The Chapel seated 200, and the congregations so increasing, the chapel was enlargened in 1874 at the rear and a school-room built on the site of the grave-yard – where several sunday school scholars were interred – thus affording accommodation for 400 people. Mr Tompkins possessed excellent begging propensities, so that he succeeded in paying off the debt for the enlargement &c. Mr Tompkins resigned in 1879 and was succeeded by the Rev E. Talbot Carter, who resigned in 1885. In this year (1885) the members numbered 180. He was succeeded by the Rev G. J. Gillingham. He came to Barking in 1883 as Secretary to the North African Mission, whose offices (local) was in Station Road, and at that time was associated with the Open-Brethren. Early in 1887 disputes arose between Mr Gillingham[391], the Deacons and Members, and in consequence Mr Gillingham resigned, and in Feburary 1887, he with some of his old members, commenced to worship in the Temperance Hall, Kings Road. (This Hall – a corrugated iron and wooden building – was erected in 1868 in the Kings Road, chiefly for temperance meetings, and at that time its members, including the Band of Hope, numbered 650. A Band of Hope meeting, held here on 30 January 1890, was the last time it was used for that purpose, and it was afterwards closed up and taken down. The cause of its closing was in consequence of the various Sunday Schools having their own Band of Hope and there was no-one to practically superintend it). He [Gillingham] was succeeded by the Rev. H. Clark, also a student from the Metropolitan Tabernacle. He was very popular, and his preaching was considered above the usual standard, consequently the Membership doubled.

During this year – 1887 – it was decided that a new building was absolutely necessary, and through the help of James Duncan Esq - a large sugar refiner of Silvertown – who gave £100 towards the project, a peice of land – 70 feet x 110 feet - was purchased in the Station Road for the purpose, and after paying for the land there was a surplus of £50. During 1888 some further alterations were made to the old chapel – viz the old ceiling & plaster was removed and replaced with match-boarding: new ventilators added: the

391 "See Salvation Army for a detailed account of Mr Gillingham and his separation from the Baptist body at Barking".

interior coloured & stenciled and other improvements at a cost of £30.10.0, and the following year (1889) by a special meeting held £113 was raised, thus making a total of £153 in the Treasurers hand. The Treasurer was the Rev C. H. Spurgeon. Mr Clark resigned in October 1891, and at his farewell, the Bible Class presented him with a handsomely bound Bible and a purse of ten-guineas by the members of the Church. He later sailed for Australia, his native place. The Rev D. H. Moore succeeded and he also hailed from the Metropolitan Tabernacle, and the membership again increased. In June 1893 a large tea-meeting was held in the old Chapel, and meetings held in aid of the contemplated new building. About 300 sat down to tea – several on account of room was refused admission, and in December 1893 a three days sale was held in the Old Chapel for the purpose of raising £100 towards the building fund. At this time there was nearly 300 members: nearly 400 attended the Sunday School and the Band of Hope numbered 220 members. Before recording the new building, the Pastors – Mr Moore – career is interesting. Previously (in 1881) he was employed in Camberwell as a common working tanner, which he left and entered the Fire-Brigade, and eventually entered the ministry.

The New Tabernacle. As stated the land was purchased in 1887 and the Memorial Stone was laid in July 1893 when the collections amounted to over £120. It is built[392] in the Grecian Renaissance style. The front is executed in best facing bricks with bath-stone dressings. Access to the building is by three different entrances. The main entrance, with its polished granite shafts and St Ann's marble bases and capitals, surmounted with a bath-stone entablature and its accessories, gives, in conjunction with the minor entrances on either side, a very pleasing effect. These enter respectively into one common lobby and into the main body of the Chapel, which admirably lighted as it is with windows glazed with Cathedral tinted glass, gives spectators the impression of being a very airy and well ventilated building. The roof, which covers a span of 40 feet, is constructed on a somewhat novel principle, it being built entirely of steel and concrete. At the further end of the Tabernacle, admirable arrangements have been made for easy access to the Vestry and other offices.

At this end of the building is the pulpit, accessible from either side, and

---

392 "This description is copied from the Local Almanack".

immediately in front is the Baptistry, the whole being situated on a slightly raised dais. There is a dado all round the building, and the seating is arranged so as to insure the best accommodation for the largest number of people. It is built to seat 600 on the ground floor and provision is made for galleries, if needed, at a later date, so that it will then accommodate 1000 persons ... the contract being for £12500. It was opened on 11th December 1893, and the opening ceremony was well attended. The meeting was conducted by the Rev C. Spurgeon (son of the Rev C. H. Spurgeon) who while addressing the congregation was continually interrupted by some person at the back of the audience, and who kept mumbling during the whole of the service. When the preacher put the question "was there anyone who loved Jesus" [the person] cried out "Yes I do as well as you". In February 1894, the paster, the Revd. H. Moore, was presented with a purse of £15. In January 1895 a fund was started for the purpose of erecting a Tablet to the memory of Mr J. Skinley - a prominent member of this body for thirty years. (For an account of this family see Churchyard). In December 1895 the Tabernacle was duly Registered for the solemnizing of marriages. In January 1897 the Rev Mr Moore resigned and was succeeded by the Revd H. S. Trueman of Chisman. In 1898 a new Schoolroom and vestries was built at the rear of the Tabernacle at a cost of £1000, and was formerly opened in October 1898 by the Rev --- Spurgeon of the Metropolitan Tabernacle. The Sunday School was continued to be held in the old Chapel, but as that building was taken over by the "Peculiar People" in 1898 the above new Schools was erected.

Dagenham Gulf. [Pages 505-508]

This noted Gulf caused through a Breach in the River Thames, was by far the most serious one that ever occurred before. The history of it is as follows.

On 17th Dec 1707[393] a strong wind – with a high tide – blew up a sluice which drained the land & it caused an immense overflow of the Thames into the marshes & it was stated officialy that had measures been taken at once to stop it – which was possible – there would probably have been no gulf now. The original breach was only 15 ft wide, but being neglected it kept increasing & reached 100 yds wide & 20 ft deep & 1000 acres of land was underwater, valued at £3 an acre. In addition 160 acres was estimated to have

---

393 *VCH Essex: vol.5*, p.286 dates the critical breach to 29th October 1707.

been swept into the sea, which caused a sand bank to form in the Thames nearly a mile in length & reached mostly accross the river. The water flowed in a zig-zag manner from Rainham Creek to near Dagenham town & back to the Thames at a spot called the "Reed ground", which appears to be in a direct line with the lane at the side of the Chequers (called Sickle Lane).

The Breach increased in the Bank from 15 ft in 1707 to 400 ft in 1714 when a Mr Boswell undertook to repair it for the sum of £16.300 but he failed[394]. (An Act was passed to repair the Breach & for 10 years from July 1714 the master of every ship or vessel coming to London was to pay 3d per ton: Coasters 3/- each voyage: Colliers 1d per chaldron – all fishing vessels were free). The next attempt was made by the famous Capt Perry in 1715[395]. In his contract dated 26 Jany 1715 the price for the work was £25000 & the work to be completed by 1st Nov 1717. This Contract also included the keeping in repair of the walls from Rainham to a spot known as the "halfway tree"[396] for 15 months afterwards. Also Capt Perry undertook to remove the sand bank from the Thames as from April 1718 which formed another contract & if his price was not sufficient he would be reccommended to Parliament.

Capt Perry encountered several obstacles. As new breaches often occurred, and his men continually struck work for higher pay, which with other accidents caused him to plead for payments of his debts. He made some very interesting discoveries. A very extensive stratum of Moor-Logg[397] was found about 4 feet below the surface of the marshes & it was about 17 ft deep & appeared to consist of whole trees & brushwoods but with very little intermixture of earth. Among the trees was the Yew of 14 in[ches] to 16 in[ches] in diameter & sound. Also Willow trees & Oak trees, together with large quantities of hazelnuts that composed this stratum. Under this was about 15 in[ches] of blue clay then gravel & sand. Capt Perry could not explain the existence of this stratum. As to the soil mentioned by Mr Perry, the general soil here to Barking Creek is composed of Blue-Clay varying in

---

394 William Boswell: *An impartial account of the frauds and abuses at Dagenham Breach and of the hardships sustained by Mr William Boswell, late undertaker of the works there, in a letter to a member of Parliament.* 1716.

395 Perry completed the essential work of repairing the Breach by 1721, so isolating the Lake or Gulf from the Thames, but it took several more years to clear the sand bank from the river. *VCH Essex: vol.5*, p.287-288.

396 A landmark on the Dagenham foreshore which was the half-way point between Gravesend and London.

depth, and nearer to the Creek – as was found in 1860 when constructing the main sewage – gravelly soil was found mostly with deposits of shells, which led the experts to beleive that at some early period it was covered by the sea.

Capt Perry ultimately completed the work but at such a great loss that the Government voted him an additional £15.000, making a total cost of £40.000. (In addition the interested landowners presented him with £1000). Some 40 Acres of land was not reclaimed & which probably comprises the body of water called the Lake. Sickle Lane connects the Lake with the Ripple Road.

The Gulf has been for many years a favorite spot for Anglers & various persons have rented the Lake for fishing purposes. Some parts of the lake is very deep – some 40 or 50 ft – and Anglers paid a fee of 1/- to fish there. Amongst the fish caught in this lake was the:- Common Carp from 10 lb[398] to 14 lb each: Tench from 1 lb: Perch 1 lb to 5 lb: Pike 12 lb to 14 lb: Carp Bream: White Bream: Hybrid Bream: Eel: Trout &c &c. In 1836 a Perch (a good size weighs 3 lb) of an unusual kind was taken here, & Mr Daniel Brandon of Chancery Lane – who then rented the Lake – forwarded it to an Expert & it was in 1837 exhibited by the Zoological Society. It measured 15 in[ches] in length: greatest depth 5 in[ches], thickness [2.5 inches] and weighed 8 lbs. But the most remarkable feature was that it was of such a different kind to what had been taken there before & at that time was rare in this Country.

About this time & some years later this spot will allways be noted for its historical associations. Mr Timbs in his Club-life of London[399] says:- On the Banks of Dagenham Lake many years since stood a Cottage[400] occupied by a princely Merchant named Preston, a Scotch Baron and MP for Dover. (Sir Robert Preston). He called it his fishing cottage & a frequent guest was the Rt Hon George Rose who also introduced Mr Pitt, the Premier who enjoyed a feast provided by Mr Preston. These three however met here Annually &

---

397 Frogley inserts a footnote regarding Moor-Logg: "Moor-Logg is a vein of divers sorts of rotten woods. What puzzled Capt Perry was how they came to be under marsh-land. (No doubt it was the work of the Romans)".

398 Pounds weight.

399 John Timbs: *Club life of London*. 2 vols. 1866.

400 Frogley has inserted a footnote: This cottage – really a small circular white house with a thatched roof – was originally rented & kept up by Gentlemen who formed fishing parties – probably the same house which in 1792 was the headquarters of a fishing Club founded by Bamber Gascoyne, Sir Edward Hulse & others. It flourished about 10 years.

from this dinner originated the famous White-bait dinner, later transferred to Greenwich (Greater London).

This house I am informed was pulled down[401] & two small houses built on its site. They were situated between the Gulf & the Thames & at that time there was a clear beautiful view of the surrounding countryside & the Kentish Hills. Around these two cottages was planted willow trees & a beautiful lawn & nearby was immense beds of reeds. In 1824 during the repairs that were being done at Plashet House Mrs Elizabeth Fry & her family took these cottages as a temporary residence when they enjoyed the fishing & boating. So enraptured was Mrs Fry with the place that the family for many years resorted there for the summer months. In 1831, in addition to her family [she] invited many friends there. These cottages has now dissappeared.

The annexed is a view of Dagenham Beach House, created by Capt Perry especially for his own observations.

In 1856 an Act of Parliament was obtained by a Company to construct Docks here[402] & about 1864 the work was commenced, but the following year gave up the enterprise for want of capital. The various large sheds they built were still standing in 1870 but in a delapidated condition. At the end of this year (1870) a jetty was built from these sheds to the Thames by a firm who started a Cartridge factory here & it projected some distance into the River[403]. This jetty was about a mile long. That portion in the river was soon shortened by a ship "The Rosetta" running into it & cutting it into two parts. This factory was really a store for cartridges & used for that purpose in 1870-1 during the Franco-Prussian War, after which the sheds were again vacated, and in 1884 they were nearly demolished by a gale.

In 1875 the Lake was acquired by the Firm of Messrs Williams & sons,

---

401 Breach House was built by Captain Perry and demolished in 1812. *VCH Essex: vol.5*, p.288-289.

402 Barking and Dagenham Libraries has Dagenham Dock Acts 1855, 1866 and 1870.

403 "The building of an ice-house, tramway and jetty in 1849 is perhaps the earliest industrial activity in the neighbourhood of Dagenham Dock. This was followed for a short time from 1872 by William Congreve's war rocket factory and then Catchpol & Co's candle factory from 1883-1895". James Howson: *A brief history of Barking and Dagenham*. 1968. p.18.

Colliery owners from Wales (Hist of Dagenham[404]) but I beleive it was in 1888 when Mr Varco Williams became possessed of the Lake & land attached, comprising about 400 Acres[405]. In addition to the Coal business he became a general trader on the Thames. Mr Samuel Williams was connected with the Thames Conservencey Board & was also President of the Master Lightermen Association & a J.P. After this purchase he began to reclaim the land & also raised the land adjacent to the river about 8 ft above the level of the Walls. The Pier and Jetties he built was connected by railway to the Southend line and a Railway Station built called "Dagenham Dock"[406] & a village is springing up. This firm also erected a bridge accross the Lake & extended Sickle Lane to the River Wall. There is there a small Gas Works, Saw Mills, Lecture Hall &c. Welsh coal is conveyed there from their collieries – a trade they are developing. The Chairman of Samuel Williams & Co is Mr Varco Williams, who in 1908 stated his firm had expended at Dagenham over £600.000. They have 275 barges & 10 steam tugs & in 1907 dealt with 1.000.000 tons of coals.

Fishing in consequence is a thing of the past – although the villagers have a little sport in this way. The latest catch of any consequence was I beleive in 1895 (March) when a Barking man fished a Pike weighing 17 lbs & measured 37 in[ches] long and 19 in[ches] in Girth. Also in December of the same year a Manor Park man landed a Pike weighing 22 lbs.

---

404 John Peter Shawcross: *History of Dagenham*. 1904. p.261. It is clear that Frogley suspected, with good reason, that Shawcross was in error in backdating the original Dagenham purchase to 1875, but hesitated to contradict him. The correct date is 1887, according to *A company's story in its setting: Samuel Williams & Sons*, 1855-1955. 1955.

405 In July 1886, Samuel Williams took his two elder sons – William Varco and Frank – into partnership, and the following year decided to purchase certain riverside lands in Dagenham. See *Residents and visitors: some Barking and Dagenham personalities*. 1992. p.34. For the development of Dagenham Dock by Samuel Williams & Sons see *A company's story in its setting: Samuel Williams & Sons, 1855-1955*. 1955.

406 Dagenham Dock station was built in 1908, after much agitation and with financial assistance from Samuel Williams & Sons Ltd.

FURTHER READING.

Barking Urban District Council. Engineer and Surveyor's Department. *List of tombstones and inscriptions at St Margaret's churchyard in the positions shown on attached plan, made from survey January to March 1930.* 1930.

Clifford, Tony *Barking and Dagenham buildings past and present.* London Borough of Barking & Dagenham, Libraries Dept, 1992.

Clifford, Tony *Barking pubs past and present.* London Borough of Barking & Dagenham, Libraries Dept, 1995.

Frogley, William Holmes *Mr Frogley's Barking: a first selection,* by Tony Clifford and Herbert Hope Lockwood. 2002.

Lockwood, Herbert Hope *Barking 100 years ago.* 1990.

Oxley, James Edwin *Barking and Ilford: an extract from the Victoria History of the County of Essex, Volume 5.* Barking & Dagenham Libraries/Redbridge Libraries, 1966, reprinted 1987.

Oxley, James Edwin *Barking vestry minutes and other parish documents.* Benham, 1955.